Freedom Fighters

Freedom Fighters

Defending Christian Freedoms in a Politically Correct Age

Rob Frost (editor)

Authentic

First published in 2005 by Authentic Media
9 Holdom Avenue, Bletchley, Milton Keynes, MK1 1QR, UK
and 129 Mobilization Drive, Waynesboro, GA 30830-4575, USA
www.authenticmedia.co.uk

British Library Cataloguing in Publication Data

A catalogue record for this book is available from
the British Library

ISBN 1-85078-613-5

The extract from the ASB 1980 is copyright © the Central Board
of Finance of the Church of England, 1980; the Archbishops'
Council, 1999 and is reproduced by permission

Cover design by Peter Barnsley
Print Management by Adare Carwin
Printed and Bound by J. H. Haynes & Co. Ltd., Sparkford

To Camille

A brilliant PA, an organiser par excellence, a truly inspiring follower of Jesus

Contents

Part 1 Perspectives

Academic Overview

Part 2 In-Depth Analysis

Acknowledgements

To Paul Conraithe for legal advice, to Mike Castle for proof-reading, to Sam Solomon for cultural advice, to Stephen Cotton for help with the manuscript and to all contributors who helped in the compilation of this book.

Foreword

As a Member of Parliament, I receive thousands of letters each year. As a Christian, I always find the letters from other Christians particularly interesting. Too often their arguments can be summarised as follows: I am a Christian, you are a Christian, this Bill is wrong, so I expect you to vote the right way, the way I see things. Confusingly, the next letter, from another Christian, may be couched in the same terms but requires me to vote the other way!

After more than twenty-five years in the House I am left with two abiding impressions. Too many believers think superficially about our faith in relation to events around us. And too many have given little thought to the fact that those who claim the name of Jesus are in a minority in our democratic society.

The common currency in both these observations from my experience is 'thinking'. In twenty-first-century Britain, the emphasis is on political correctness, dumbing down and sound bites. Nevertheless ideas, thinking through issues and developing philosophical frameworks for what we believe and say remain crucial.

St Paul was right. The predominant pressure of our age is the world seeking to squeeze us into its mould. Our willingness and ability to resist are a measure of our faith.

The world's belief system, when translated into relational behaviour, is relativistic. It eschews ideas of good and evil, and often the very idea of right and wrong. Instead, the criteria focus on whether anyone else is 'hurt' by a course of action, and whether behaviour can be excused on the grounds that worse behaviour can be found in others. The assumption is that acts between consenting adults are fine and no one else's business. The world's definition of the common good seldom has an explicitly Christian or moral dimension.

We Christians, on the other hand, affirm that our authority stems from God and his word, not from political parties, single interest pressure groups, riches or sex. It was Isaiah who, at God's urging, said 'woe' to those who call evil good. And it was Peter, when his liberty and maybe even his life were in jeopardy, who insisted that he must obey God rather than men.

Good and evil, right and wrong are moral concepts. So the battle to define them is fought out over the source of our authority and hence our presuppositions.

We believe in the need for men and women to have a new, restored relationship with God and we believe that this can be achieved only in and through Jesus. The cross is the symbol of our Authority. And the relationships which stem from it are different and distinct from their secular counterparts.

The world adopts relative standards because individuals do not have the inner, spiritual power to succeed when judged in an absolute, divine framework.

Yet it is so easy to succumb to the contemporary pressure to conform. Standing out, sticking up for what you believe when in a minority – sometimes of one – takes more self-confidence and inner strength than many of us possess. It is easier to go with the crowd.

The consequences of this form of anonymity are all around us. The selfish, violent behaviour which characterises our communities is what happens when we cede the battle of ideas and beliefs. Violent crime increases. Nearly half of babies are born out of wedlock. A quarter of our youngsters claim to have committed a crime.

The majority do not share our Christian presuppositions and so their rootless standards of behaviour prevail. Our Authority is replaced by no authority. Even the law does not claim to be an ultimate authority. At best it constrains behaviour. Only Jesus Christ can fundamentally change human beings.

We are the 'salt' which preserves society. If we withdraw, if we do not fight to be heard and to influence, rot sets in. As Edmund Burke reminds us, all that is necessary for evil to prevail is for good men (and women) to do nothing.

But, you say, we are a minority. The majority do not reflect our presuppositions, so they will always 'win' in a democracy. In the absolute sense, this is true. But in practice I have discovered that it does not have to be true. There are others who, on a specific issue, may want what we want. Our belief systems may differ but our ends may coincide.

How difficult it is to galvanise Christians to see the world in this pragmatic way. I am no less a Christian if I work side by side with a Muslim or an atheist to achieve what, for different 'theological' but identical social reasons, we both want to achieve. This is what we need to do in a democracy in order to achieve a majority.

We are about values and our values are being traduced. Our systems and language are being undermined to produce results we reject.

Take 'tolerance' as an example – a prime Christian virtue. Today, tolerance as a value is used to permit and condone whatever action people wish to pursue. So we who have beliefs stemming from Divine Authority are no longer the epitome of tolerance. Indeed we are depicted as 'intolerant' when we seek to affirm the truth or inhibit the unacceptable behaviour of others.

In America the moral dimension of politics was the single most potent force in the election of a President. In Europe, with British MEPs joining in, a potential European Commissioner was rejected out of hand because he aligned himself with the teaching of the church on homosexuality.

So much for 'tolerance'.

This book seeks to explore the many facets of these issues – not least from the everyday experience of many Christians. I hope it will inspire you, as it should.

I also hope it will challenge you. All of us need to be confronted with that challenge anew and to be given the determination to rise to meet it, in Jesus' name.

Sir Brian Mawhinney MP

Introduction

Thirty years ago, when I was a student at theological college, the Principal called me into his office and asked me to look after a young Macedonian minister called Kitan, who had come to the UK for further study. He spoke little English, and was struggling to cope with the many pressures of university life.

Kitan became a close friend, and over the course of the year I learnt much about his struggles back home. He had been frequently hassled by the police, forbidden to hold evangelistic meetings, and sometimes interrogated and imprisoned for his illegal church-planting activities in a sensitive communist state. He preached for an hour at funerals because this was one of the few occasions when he could speak freely, without threat of imprisonment.

At the end of our year together, a group of us theological students took Kitan back home to Macedonia in our twelve-year-old minibus. It was a very long journey and a great adventure, during which we pushed it up the Alps! Later, at a secret 'smuggling depot' in Trieste we filled it with 'illegal' Macedonian Bibles for the churches of that troubled land.

Approaching the border and waiting for the guards to search us for illegal contraband was one of the most frightening experiences of my life. They took the car in front of us to pieces, but then simply waved us through without seeing the 'illegal' stock of Bibles stacked high on our vehicle's seats. Our prayer to 'make seeing eyes blind' was clearly answered that day!

We distributed those Bibles early one morning, deep in a forest. Christians appeared through the mist, desperate for their own copy of the Word of God. I have never forgotten them, nor the evident persecution which they endured for the sake of the Gospel.

Over the following years Kitan witnessed the collapse of communism, the legalisation of evangelism and the meteoric rise to Prime Minister of one of his church congregation. So much changed so quickly.

Recently I was appointed President of Release International, an organisation which cares for the persecuted church around the world. This work has brought me into renewed contact with Christians in different parts of the world who are under the pressure of persecution from many quarters.

This work led me to think more about the society in which I live and minister, and to begin to consider how contemporary societal trends are affecting Christian life and witness in the UK. Gradually, and with a great deal of personal concern, I have concluded that the erosion of Christian freedom in the UK is accelerating so quickly that unless British Christians begin to act together we will be facing persecution here before the end of my active ministry.

I will never forget Kitan preaching in the open air in this country, tears streaming down his face, as he recognised that he could never do it in his own. Could it be that, even now, he would find such an activity almost impossible?

You must weigh for yourself the evidence of the witnesses whose words you will read in these pages. Those nearer the beginning of the book are more experiential in their view, and those towards the end are more academic. I hope that in this chorus of different voices and experiences you will find much to make you think ... and much to stimulate you to pray.

Rob Frost

Part 1
Perspectives

Contents

Part 1 Perspectives

Chapter 1

The Evangelist: Rob Frost

Rob Frost is the Director of Share Jesus International, an interdenominational ministry supported by the main denominational churches of the UK. Rob is also the leader of the *Easter People* Christian conference, and directs a large mission programme each summer. Author of twenty-six books and producer of ten theatrical productions, he presents a Sunday morning chat show on Premier Radio and hosts a series on an international satellite television station. Rob is married to Jacqui and they have two sons, Andy and Chris.

Free to belong

Sometimes I feel as though I'm drowning in a sea of political correctness. Don't get me wrong; I'm convinced that anti-discrimination legislation has done much good, and that vulnerable groups have been afforded much-needed protection. In that way 'political correctness' has been a force for good. But there can be negative outcomes, too. A society which seeks too much control over what its population thinks, says and does can eventually become a tyranny, a place where free speech is a distant memory and the 'thought police' investigate anyone who isn't part of the dominant majority.

Take, for instance, the work of a group which called itself Faiths Together on Campus. It was a partnership of liberal-minded people such as the Catholic Student Council, the Federation of Student Islamic Societies, the National Union of Students, the Union of Jewish Students and the Student Christian Movement.

This strange grouping gathered round an agenda which threatened the existence of hundreds of Christian Unions on campuses across the UK.

Faiths Together on Campus aimed to bring together Catholic, Islamic, Christian, Jewish, Hindu and Sikh societies at universities in an attempt to create religious 'tolerance and respect'. It seemed a very politically correct and well-intentioned thing to do.

The draft paper produced by this group, however, lumped Christian Unions and the Christian Medical Fellowship together with cults which use brainwashing techniques. It argued that because these evangelical Christian organisations insisted that student leaders assent to a doctrinal statement, they were flouting the 1998 Human Rights Act.

The paper argued that this doctrinal test enabled extreme factions to keep a 'stranglehold' on certain student religious societies, and that it stifled varied opinions. This group intended to 'monitor religious toleration on campuses' and produced a 'Code of Practice' that insisted that no religious organisation should discriminate in its rules for either membership or leadership on grounds of religious belief!

Thank goodness that public opinion and extensive publicity in the Christian media led to the demise of this ill-founded initiative. Those behind Faiths Together on Campus should have realised that Article 9 of the European Convention on Human Rights gives all religions the right to propagate their faith.

Such a high-profile group should have known that Section 43 of the Education Act of 1986 gives religious groups protection to engage in evangelism because it is a form of freedom of speech. They should have known that British law recognises the principle of freedom of association. One of our rights is to exclude people from our organisations if they do not subscribe to our fundamental principles. One simply can't imagine a similar group called Politics Together on Campus trying to ensure that the Socialist Society could be led by a Tory!

Above all, they should have realised that one of the foundations of our British culture is the Magna Carta of 1215, which says, 'We . . . have confirmed for us and our heirs in perpetuity that the English Church shall be free and shall have its right undiminished and its liberties unimpaired.' This group failed to understand some of the basic foundations of our religious freedoms. Their work seems typical of so many initiatives which start out as very well-meaning.

This political correctness threatens our right to nominate our chosen leaders to Christian organisations and to employ Christians in key roles in the life of the church. We need to speak out about it, and to begin to mobilise the Christian voice in the UK.

Free to believe

Similar well-intentioned ideas were put forward by the former Home Secretary, David Blunkett, in his emergency measures to counter terrorism following the '9/11' attacks in the USA. The House of Commons debated these measures on 19 November 2001.

In that debate Mr Blunkett said, 'The argument is not whether people should be allowed to say what they want but whether the intention, and the likely effect, of their comments is to stir up racial hatred.' This was a very well-intentioned statement, and I would stand with David Blunkett in his abhorrence of any action which would 'stir up racial hatred'. But, if it were carried too far, this legislation could actually lead to a diminution of religious rights. In the same debate Sir Brian Mawhinney said, '(The Home Secretary) will know, to use his own words, that two of the central foundations of the Christian faith – namely, that Jesus Christ was both man and God and that people can get into a relationship with God only through Jesus Christ – are deemed by some in other religions to be insulting and offensive. Indeed, in some countries it is so insulting and offensive that the very statement of Christian faith is enough to put someone in prison.' Sir Brian aptly summed up my own concerns.

Evangelical Christians have found some strange allies in their concern about this legislation. The comedian Rowan Atkinson has condemned the proposed law on the grounds that it would make priests, vicars and Christians exempt from portrayal by comics and cartoonists. I believe that he's right. A healthy society encourages free speech, and along with that comes the right to publicly question the activities of every religious group.

The National Secular Society was also concerned that a section of the 2001 emergency anti-terrorism legislation came close to creating an 'all religions' blasphemy law, allowing judges to impose a sentence of up to seven years if an offence was found to be aggravated by motives of religious hatred. Mr Porteous Wood of the Society concluded that the offence, which in penalty terms would be on a par with racially aggravated crimes, was a cause for concern because of its impact on the freedom of speech.

Christians in the UK should be concerned that this legislation has now passed its second reading and is beyond the committee stage in the House of Commons. Particularly so, in the light of the experience of Pastor Nalliah and Pastor Scot, two Christian leaders in Melbourne, Australia.

They hosted a seminar for 250 Christians on the theme of Islam, as part of the teaching ministry of Melbourne Pentecostal Church called Catch the Fire Ministries. The content of this conference was reported to the Equal Opportunities Commission. The legal case which stemmed from this complaint led to a test case involving the Islamic Council of Victoria versus Catch The Fire Ministries. It has cost more than $1 million in legal fees and appears to have achieved little but growing enmity between different religious groups. Both ministers were found guilty by the court in December 2004.

Leading politician Peter Costello, tipped by some to be a future Australian Prime Minister, referred to the case in a speech in May 2004, when he said

> I do not think that we should resolve differences about religious views in our community with lawsuits between the

different religions. Nor do I think that the object of religious harmony will be promoted by organising witnesses to go along to the meetings of other religions to collect evidence for the purpose of later litigation.

The action which has been taken under this new law, the time, the cost, the extent of the proceedings and the remedies that are available all illustrate, in my view, that this is a bad law. Even if, as the judge suggested in his summing up of the trial, both pastors were guilty of giving an unbalanced view of the Islamic religion, I find it hard to accept such a ruling in a country known for its traditions of free speech. The effect on the Christian ministers, who claim that the information shared was just factual, cannot be easily estimated. 'This has caused us a tremendous amount of time and stress,' the head of Catch the Fire Ministries, Pastor Danny Nalliah, said in a press release. I would agree with Costello when he concluded

> Tolerance under the law is a great part of this tradition. Tolerance does not mean that all views are the same. It does not mean that differing views are equally right. What it means is that where there are differences, no matter how strongly held, different people will respect the right of others to hold them.

If the experience of our Christian friends in Australia is to be replicated here, we will see a rapid deterioration of what has been a creative and healthy culture of interfaith dialogue. The introduction of 'religious hatred' legislation in the UK will do nothing to improve race relations. Former Home Secretary David Blunkett's press statement in defence of his proposals certainly did nothing to allay the concerns of many evangelical Christians when he said

> We need to be able to take on those extremists and say I'm afraid in our society, pluralism and openness, the ability to accept differences without being subsumed, is crucial to our survival, it's what distinguishes all of us, from every faith, from those who take our lives because they reject our faith, and it applies equally from far right evangelical Christians to extremists in the Islamic faith.

Graham Wood, writing in *The Church of England Newspaper*, observed

> Mr Blunkett was equating evangelicals with Islamic terrorists who want to kill those who do not share their faith. Are evangelicals on the same level as Osama bin Laden in some way? What, or who, is referred to in that favourite political slogan 'the extremists'?

Free to evangelise

Thirty years ago, when I first worked in hospital chaplaincy, I was welcomed as a member of the medical team. I was given access to confidential information and notified of every new admission. In many hospitals this is now a thing of the past, and chaplains must trudge the wards 'blind' because information legislation prevents them from knowing who might appreciate a visit. I recognise that patients should be given the right to choose whether they are visited by a chaplain or not, but in many hospitals this is now not even an option.

Thirty years ago I regularly preached in the open air, and the relevant 'permit' was usually granted as a formality. My experience in recent days is that this kind of permission is not as forthcoming as it once was.

Thirty years ago I would not have thought twice about sharing my faith with a Muslim, a Buddhist or a Sikh, and in fact did so on many occasions. The dialogue and friendship which emanated from such conversations was, to me, a hallmark of living in a healthy multicultural society. I would certainly think twice about doing this today, just in case the person I was talking to took offence. In my view a healthy society is one which encourages dialogue and is a place where public debate is a mark of its freedom, the kind of society in which a Buddhist, a Muslim or an atheist has the right to talk to me about their worldview in the same way as I have the right to share mine.

I have led evangelistic missions in scores of towns and cities throughout the United Kingdom. Some of these have been in areas with large Asian populations, such as Bradford, Southall and the Lancashire mill towns. In these missions we have often partnered with Asian congregations and seen how the joint witness of Christians from British and Asian backgrounds has been a powerful witness to multiculturalism and a high-profile example of good race relations in action. In hundreds of personal contacts between our teams and local people I have never received a single complaint.

Recently a mainstream church denomination refused to welcome our mission teams to Birmingham because this activity was considered 'inappropriate' for such a multicultural context. One church leader informed me that the arrival of such teams would be 'derogatory to good race relations', even though we had promised that all the teams would receive racism awareness training and would be multicultural in their mix.

Does this mean that the UK is now subdivided into areas 'suitable for Christian mission' and others which are too sensitive or too multicultural? And if so, what does this say about the future of evangelism in the UK and the freedom of religious expression which I thought was an integral part of a pluralist culture?

Free to practise

While I am not particularly enthusiastic about the hijab as a form of dress for Islamic women, I was deeply concerned to read of the French government's plan to ban this head-covering from the school classroom.

I was also worried that the same legislation could make the wearing of a large crucifix illegal. The Sikh turban and the Jewish skullcap are included in the same provisions within the French education system.

There are some who would support similar rules within the British context. This drive towards secularisation seems to be getting ever stronger. Those of us in the Free churches who don't wear the skullcap, turban, hijab or crucifix should not imagine that new French laws don't concern us. We are part of the European Union, and decisions such as this made by one member state can become very influential in the political processes of others. Any limitation of religious freedom is, for me, the thin end of a very large wedge.

Article 9 of the European Convention states that everyone has the right to freedom of thought, conscience and religion. This right includes the freedom to change one's religion or belief and the freedom, either alone or in community with others and in public or in private, to manifest one's religion or belief in worship, teaching, practice or observance.

If the wearing of religious symbols is not part of our freedom to 'manifest religion in public', what is? Though we might not share the religious perspectives or belief systems of the groups affected by this French legislation, we should still stand with them in the protection of their basic religious rights.

I was encouraged to see Cherie Blair defending the right of Shabina Begum to wear an Islamic jilbab instead of her school uniform. This girl was excluded from a high school in Luton. Lord Justice Brooks said that the case had raised the question of whether a child with sincere religious beliefs should be able to challenge school uniform policy.

In the creation passages of Genesis 1 and 2 we see that human dignity stems from the fact that we are created in the image of God. Because of this, all human beings are worthy of respect, regardless of their abilities, status, race or gender. In our faith context we believe that all are equally worthy and equally sinful, and we believe that it is God's will that we should all be saved. We understand that God created human beings with an innate freedom to choose how they live, and we respect that God-given freedom of choice which is part of being human.

I respect the right of women to wear the hijab, of schoolgirls to wear the jilbab, and of young people to wear large crucifixes as part of their religious observance, but I also expect people to respect my right, and the right of Christian schoolkids, to wear a fish badge or to carry the Bible in public. I would say that I have every right to display the symbols of my belief system because I am a member of a free and tolerant society.

Article 9 of the European Convention on Human Rights states that

> Freedom to manifest one's religion or beliefs shall be subject only to such limitations as are prescribed by law and are necessary in a democratic society in the interests of public safety, for the protection of public order, health or morals, or the protection of the rights and freedoms of others.

In view of the words of this European convention it seems particularly ironic that Rocco Buttiglione, a prominent and conservative Roman Catholic, caused a constitutional crisis when he was almost appointed European Commissioner for Justice.

In one of the committee hearings regarding his appointment he said that he regarded homosexuality as a sin. This former philosophy professor and friend of the Pope affirmed, 'I have the right to think that homosexuality is a sin. But this has no effect on politics because in politics the principle of non-discrimination prevails.'

Buttiglione, whose nomination put in jeopardy the appointment of the entire commission, claimed that he had been the victim of 'an anti-Catholic inquisition'. Does this mean that a conservative Roman Catholic is no longer welcome in the corridors of European power? Could he not practise his faith and still uphold principles of justice and equality? Should he be expected to keep his religious views to himself simply to get the job?

Free to educate

Thirty years ago I would not have thought twice about the content of my talk in a school assembly. I would have considered it basic that I could refer to Jesus as Christ, divide time into the eras AD and BC, speak of miracles and of salvation, and express my heartfelt belief that he is the only way to God.

In a multicultural and multifaith context I would be considered reckless to do the same today! It would appear that these freedoms are now being questioned – even in church schools.

I find it of deep personal concern that even the worship activities of church schools are coming under greater scrutiny. Nick Cohen, writing in the *New Statesman*, suggested that the use of 'meditation disciplines' published in class notes by the Diocese of Canterbury was similar to 'hypnosis'.

I listened with great interest to BBC Radio 4's *Today* programme as the Right Rev Kenneth Stevenson, Bishop of Portsmouth and Chair of the Church of England Board of Education, had to rebut accusations that these activities were similar to 'brainwashing' techniques.

Christian meditation has been an integral part of the church's spiritual discipline since the days of the early Church Fathers, and I find it deplorable that the church's right to encourage it in church schools and in religious education lessons is being questioned.

In recent years, there has been an increasing suspicion about the ethos and growth of church schools. In 2003 the Archbishop of Canterbury defended Muslim and other faith schools and insisted they were 'nothing to apologise for'. Dr Rowan Williams said the 'good following wind' for faith schools had, regrettably, changed after 9/11.

In his first major speech on education after taking up his post, Dr Williams said Muslims and members of other faiths should be able to continue to set up their own schools, which are eligible for state funding and support. I completely support Dr Williams in this proposal, which is another indication of a free and flourishing society.

Dr Williams described sharply contrasting approaches to education. 'There is a real tension in educational thinking between those whose concern is primarily, almost exclusively, with imparting skills to individuals and those who understand education as something that forms the habits of living in a group, identifying common aspirations and making possible cooperation and conversation.' The ethos of church schools was of the latter type, he stressed.

We can only hope and pray that the 'good following wind' behind the growth and development of Christian and church-based schools will return. Such schools have much to add to the richness and quality of our education system.

Free to be

When Alexis de Tocqueville wrote *Democracy in America* he concluded that there can be a 'tyranny of the majority'. De Tocqueville observed that

> democratic majorities can significantly oppress minorities, indulging in tyrannical activities of suppression and expropriation. Moreover, this could all, in a democracy, be apparently legal since a thoroughgoing democratic state would

subordinate all avenues of redress and protection to the majority.

In other words, do the majority have the right to suppress the views of the minority? Christian lawyer Michael Ovey, writing about the 'tyranny of majorities', concluded that

> Christians cannot give unqualified commitments to obey majorities. If they did, that amounts to saying the majority has no 'overlord' and either derives its power legitimacy from something other than God or simply from itself. Such absolute commitments amount to complicity in the tyranny – to use the word in an extended sense – of majoritarian supremacy.

Jesus Christ was a radical revolutionary and his initial followers were a tiny minority. As we in the UK rediscover what it means to be a tiny minority, we must not make the mistake of thinking that the majority is always right. On the contrary, we need to rediscover what it means to be salt and light, and how we can affect the whole even though we are vastly outnumbered. As we become an identified 'minority' within the UK population we must leave behind the old assumptions about our importance, influence and prestige and move towards a new role and a new opportunity.

We must become more outspoken. We must challenge those ideas and popular trends which are unbiblical and dangerous. This may lead us into direct conflict with political institutions, societal structures and legal authorities; and some of us may find this a costly activity. Just because we are a minority, it does not mean that we are excluded from the rights and privileges of any minority group within a pluralist society. In fact, it is time we began to make a claim on those rights which are fairly ours. We have the right of freedom of speech and we have a right to believe, to worship, to serve and to proselytise.

Perhaps it's time we began to claim 'our rights'. For in the babble of voices claiming 'justice' for their particular cause, faith community or sexual orientation, the Christian church has often been silent and invisible. We have an historic right of freedom of speech, which means that we should be able to proclaim the uniqueness and divinity of Jesus Christ in the pulpit, in the street and through printed and electronic media without let or hindrance.

We have a responsibility to protect these rights not only for ourselves, but also for other religious groups and minorities. And, as you will read in the concluding section of this book, we have a Christian imperative to ensure that everything we do or say is motivated by love and carried through in the grace and compassion which we find in Jesus.

2

The Police Inspector: Bob Pull

Bob Pull was born in north-east England and is an Inspector in the Metropolitan Police, based at New Scotland Yard. After a varied career including community and public order policing, he now spearheads initiatives alongside faith communities, building trust and confidence with police, and has recently trained street pastors in South London. In September 2004, Bob stepped down from leading the Christian Police Association (Metropolitan Branch) to undertake training as a Baptist Minister at Spurgeon's College. Bob is married to Gill, with two grown-up children.

Halcyon days

'Delta Romeo from 152, VDU check 152, over.' There I was, standing on a street in west London, speaking into my personal radio (PR) in order to establish the ownership of a vehicle during a stop in the street.

The year was 1977 and I was police constable 152DR, armed with the latest technology: a notebook, a wooden stick, a whistle and, strapped to my body, a clumpy PR that sometimes worked.

It was my first opportunity to do a vehicle check using a computer – the Visual Display Unit. But if I needed to do a check on previous convictions it meant a phone call to New Scotland Yard. A manual search of the million paper files at the Criminal Records Office would then commence.

The law that I used regularly for 'stop and search' was Section 4 of the Vagrancy Act 1824. This contained the 'sus' law, hated by ethnic minority communities and young people. More widely used was Section 66 of the Metropolitan Police Act 1839, a catch-all law enabling stop and search of anybody for almost anything.

The 'sus' law enabled police officers to arrest and charge suspected persons or reputed thieves if they made three attempts at committing an offence. In response to public outcry, it was replaced by the Criminal Attempts Act 1988, which strangely only required two attempts to make the individual liable to arrest.

Details of stops were entered in a large book kept in the front office of the police station. This book was checked by the collator, who updated the card index on local criminals, and of course by my reporting sergeant, who had the awful habit of addressing me as 'Rosie'; the name of a rookie cop popular on television at that time.

I'd never used a typewriter before, and my first update of a criminal record took me eight hours of one-finger typing. My beady-eyed supervisor had ordered me to retype it ten times before it received his seal of approval.

'If only technology could help,' I said to myself. 'Things would be so much better and easier. Perhaps a computer that could do all my paperwork. I would then get it right every time.'

All change

Times did change over the next twenty years. There were riots at the Notting Hill Carnival, in Brixton, and during the miners' strike. Where police had once used dustbin lids for protection, they were now supplied with plastic shields, crash helmets, fire-resistant overalls, CS spray and extendible batons. Police carrying firearms became a common sight. My trusty, rarely used wooden truncheon was now inadequate and outdated.

A number of events – the Iranian Embassy siege, the IRA's bombing activity, and the murders of police officers outside Harrods and the Libyan Embassy, on the Broadwater Farm estate, in Brixton and elsewhere – contributed to the urgent necessity for police to be more technologically advanced. The murder of Stephen Lawrence and the subsequent allegation of institutional racism against the police by Sir William Macpherson[1] forced a change of police behaviour and in the way the police go about their business. Laws enacted in the eighteenth and early nineteenth centuries also needed to change in response to advances in technology and changes in society.

The most noteworthy change in respect of the rights of the individual was the Police and Criminal Evidence Act 1984. In hindsight this perhaps has an Orwellian feel in terms of both its date and the systems and processes it covers. Every part of police activity has been influenced by this legislation.

The police in turn have become increasingly sophisticated in respect of data handling. Virtually everything from the decision-making process for arrest through to charging a person with a criminal offence is now recorded. Initially this was done by means of handwritten records, but more recently video and audio recording equipment has been installed in police vehicles, police station confines and custody areas.

Litigation, legislation, complaints against police, reductions in conviction rates and high-profile miscarriages of justice drove these changes through. I agree that there is a need for accountability and for the formalisation of police powers, but accountability also imposes a requirement to collect more and more data about individuals. Anti-discriminatory legislation in particular requires data to be collected on ethnicity, gender and, more recently, sexual orientation and religious affiliation.

Getting the balance right

There is a fine balance between evidential integrity, security and civil liberties. Has this balance now shifted, to the point where individual rights and freedoms are becoming restricted?

Some criminals are extremely adept at devising the next scam. They plan their work in an attempt to secure the maximum gain and to avoid detection. Terrorists in particular will now go to extraordinary lengths to achieve their objectives. It is no longer the case that terrorists are concerned about their safety. More individuals are prepared to give their life as part of the plan.

The police and security services have of necessity risen to this challenge, using cutting-edge technology to aid the prevention and detection of crimes. Waiting for an incident to happen is not an option. It is essential to intervene at an early stage to prevent atrocities.

New and proposed legislation on the prevention of terrorism will under some circumstances deny individuals the right to trial by jury. Foreign nationals can now be detained indefinitely without trial on the evidence of the security services alone. If the fundamental right of trial by jury is abandoned, how can citizens be absolutely certain that justice is being carried out in these cases?

I understand the dilemma, but I remain concerned that recent emergency legislation, combined with the merging of computer data from a number of sources, will pave the way for even more surveillance of everyday lives, beyond that justified by the threat of terrorism. Rights and freedoms are becoming increasingly restricted under the banner of counter-terrorism. Surely the basic human rights of detainees need some judicial overview?

Identity cards

Richard Thomas, Britain's Information Commissioner, has warned that proposed legislation on identity cards for UK citizens and other measures could lead to the creation of a 'Big Brother state'. If plans for ID cards, a population register and a database recording information about every child from birth to adulthood go ahead, he argued, we could find ourselves 'sleepwalking' into a surveillance society where unacceptably large amounts of information are gathered on each citizen.

In part these measures are a response to the increased threat of terrorism, the increasing occurrence of child abuse, and an unquenchable thirst for statistics on the part of the Government, but they could cause new problems.

I'm no stranger to carrying ID; after all, my police warrant card is always in my pocket, as are my assorted credit, loyalty and membership cards. I accept that an ID card could in fact be useful in reducing the amount of identification we need to carry.

David Blunkett, then Home Secretary, said in a speech to the Institute of Public Policy Research in November 2004

> The ability to prove one's identity reliably is an ever more important aspect of modern life. A national ID cards scheme will provide a 'gold standard' for doing that, protecting individuals from the modern-day crime of identity theft, protecting public services for use by those who are properly entitled to them, and helping us tackle crime, terrorism, and illegal immigration and working.

It is still difficult to believe that this 'gold standard' of identification will prevent terrorism or identity theft. The latter crime could actually be made easier. Sophisticated criminals are already targeting cash machines with electronic gadgetry that reads debit card magnetic strips, and getting access to people's internet bank account security information. It won't be long before the new 'chip and PIN' security is also breached. It is proposed that ID cards will eventually become compulsory by law. Failing to produce a card on the request of a police officer or government official will, despite current assurances, become a criminal offence. Cards will be stolen or mislaid and fall into the wrong hands. The very card that is meant to protect individuals could also effectively criminalise them.

An oppressive future government could also use the ID card system to prevent access to services or restrict movement as a form of punishment for those who express views contrary to the party line or who engage in other 'unacceptable' behaviour.

George Orwell, writing over half a century ago about his chilling vision of the future, captures my concerns

> All their ferocity was turned outwards, against the enemies of the State, against foreigners, traitors, saboteurs, thought-criminals. It was almost normal for people over thirty to be frightened of their own children. And with good reason, for hardly a week passed in which The Times did not carry a paragraph describing how some eavesdropping little sneak – 'child hero' was the phrase generally used – had overheard some compromising remark and denounced its parents to the Thought Police.[2]

I am not a conspiracy or apocalypse theorist. My observations are drawn from my experience of the world around me and from my occupation. There has never been a time in history when there has been so much intrusion into the everyday activities of the population.

Advances in technology and a strong criminal law do of course have significant benefits. But conversely, in the wrong hands and without stringent safeguards these may lead to a severe curtailment of individual liberties.

Christianity in a secular society

At this point you may be thinking, why should we fear? We are Christians; we don't do anything wrong! Alister McGrath argues that in a secular society

> it is implied that to defend Christianity is to belittle non-Christian religions, which is unacceptable in a multicultural society. Especially to those of liberal political convictions, the multicultural agenda demands that religions should not be permitted to make truth claims, to avoid the dangers of imperialism and triumphalism. Indeed, there seems to be a widespread perception that rejection of religious pluralism entails intolerance or unacceptable claims to exclusivity.[3]

I enjoy working with and engaging with people from diverse religions, cultures and lifestyles. I don't always agree with everything other people do or believe. When I talk with others, sometimes what they say will sway my opinions and sometimes my view will remain constant.

My thoughts and opinions are the very centre of my being, shaped by experience, by spirituality and through my reading of the Bible. Open debate is increasingly being squeezed by a secular agenda. It is becoming difficult to speak about some Christian principles. My thoughts often remain just thoughts because I fear I will be misinterpreted.

Popular opinion changes the moral landscape in a secular society. Abortion is generally accepted as a form of contraception. Foxhunting with hounds is banned as it is deemed to be cruel. Prevailing attitudes and moral shifts in society have an impact on legislation.

Christians in our secular society are often marginalised. I have dealt with over twenty cases in which Christian colleagues have been subjected to discrimination in the workplace. There is an increasing reliance on the law to prevent legitimate debate of Christian values. In various circumstances Christians run the risk of an allegation of hate crime.

For example, police investigated comments made by Peter Forster, Bishop of Chester, in the *Chester Chronicle* newspaper[4] in 2003 about the possibility of some people who are 'primarily homosexual' 'reorientating' themselves with psychiatric help. The Crown Prosecution Service advised in this instance that no criminal offence had been committed. If he had made his comments in the street the matter could have been in breach of the Public Order Act 1986. In an ever-shifting political environment there is a fine balance between legitimate debate and a criminal offence.

Article 9 of The European Convention on Human Rights says

> Everyone has the right to freedom of thought, conscience and religion; this right includes freedom to change his religion or belief, and freedom, either alone or in community with others and in public or private, to manifest his religion or belief, in worship, teaching, practice and observance.

> Freedom to manifest one's religion or beliefs shall be subject only to such limitations as are prescribed by law and are necessary in a democratic society in the interests of public safety, for the protection of public order, health or morals, or the protection of the rights and freedoms of others.

But how long will some Christian practices and beliefs remain a freedom? Will they be limited by laws that reflect shifting, non-biblical morals? Even the second paragraph above could possibly allow this.

Use of the expression 'Love the sinner but hate the sin' in certain contexts could place a Christian outside the law. Calling someone a sinner can be deemed sufficiently offensive or threatening, or regarded as causing such harassment or alarm, that criminal proceedings are a possibility. Street preachers are particularly at risk of arrest if someone complains to police that they are offended by what is said.

New technology

Digital photographic and audio equipment is so versatile that cameras and microphones less than the size of a buttonhole are available. Covert surveillance of criminals and terrorists also involves satellite tracking and other eavesdropping equipment. A trip to Tottenham Court Road, London, will suffice to show you the remarkable range of electronic gadgetry that is available off the shelf.

Some cameras are equipped to recognise the profiles of individuals within crowds. This has a significant use in combating football hooliganism and terrorism. Some companies are now testing it with a view to enabling staff to access buildings or offices without having to use a swipe card.

Automatic number plate recognition systems are capable of scouring national police databases within seconds and establishing who is the registered keeper of a vehicle. Just try travelling into the congestion zone in the centre of London during restricted hours without paying, and you'll soon find your fine landing on your doorstep.

'Truth' software is now used in the insurance and financial sectors. When we telephone an insurance company the call is most likely recorded for training purposes and security. Our answers to questions are often subjected to a set of truth tests. If the tone of our reply gives rise to doubt concerning our authenticity, insurance cover or other services could be refused. This technology is at present only used as an indicator of untruthfulness. I am concerned, however, that one day it may be accepted without question as evidence in a criminal court.

Fingerprint and iris recognition technology has improved to the point that people stopped in the street can be readily identified if they have a criminal record. Banks are considering using iris technology for cash machine users: instead of entering your PIN, you'll have your eyes scanned.

Foreseeable dangers

I am not against the use of technology to keep communities and individuals safe from crime. There are enormous advantages in terms of personal security crime investigation, detection and prevention. The increased use of closed-circuit television (CCTV), however, has become worryingly intrusive. It is currently used for revenue raising and security, but this is just the beginning. Every journey we take in our cars may in the future be logged. Beyond this there is a possibility that CCTV could be used to monitor individuals or their vehicles and restrict them from entering various premises or areas. This again is a good thing for security, but will Christians be restricted from preaching in the future?

The Anti-Social Behaviour Act 2003, which is designed for dealing with anti-social behaviour of various types, can also place restrictions on people's lives. It provides powers for the police in conjunction with local authorities to apply to courts to restrain individuals, close premises, impose parenting orders and generally take action to control a minority of offenders who cause severe disruption to our lives.

But such orders are also being used for other reasons. For example, Camden Council in London served advertising executives working for two major record companies with Anti-Social Behaviour Orders (ASBOs) for fly-posting in the borough, after local residents complained about their illegal adverts. One could imagine, in theory, the possibility of similar action being taken against street preachers who refuse to stop preaching or handing out Bibles – having their Bibles confiscated and their movements restricted, and perhaps even receiving a prison sentence.

ASBOs can be used to prevent individuals entering defined areas or to prevent the possession of certain items. They demand a relatively low level of proof and are granted on the balance of probabilities, including hearsay evidence (evidence of a third party who is not a witness).

New proposed legislation making incitement to cause religious hatred an offence should also make Christians sit up and take notice. While some of the fears expressed by Christians are perhaps exaggerated, there are nevertheless grounds for concern about the direction the Government is taking.

Non-Christian faith communities are pressing for protection and see this law as an avenue of hope. The reality may be something completely different, however, with clerics of these faiths also being investigated if their views are not compatible with liberal secular morality.

Foreseeable possibilities

Knowing the criminal justice system as I do, watching the emergence of new legislation and the rapid development of information technology, and also recognising an increasing intolerance towards Christianity and other faiths, I suspect that Christians and other religious communities will have difficulties in freely practising their faith in the future. While some may not be too bothered about the possible demise of street preaching and door-to-door evangelism, the message from the pulpit could be the next of our freedoms to be jeopardised.

I foresee technology becoming increasingly intrusive and laws more Draconian. Tolerance will be defined within a liberal secular, morally shifting agenda, which will effectively mean intolerance towards some faith communities. Personal freedoms will continue to be eroded.

The fine balance between security and civil liberties has tipped away from freedom.

---

[1] *The Stephen Lawrence Inquiry*, report (London: The Stationery Office, 1999).

[2] Orwell, George, *Nineteen Eighty-Four* (London: Secker & Warburg, 1949).

[3] McGrath, Alister, *Bridge-Building* (Leicester: IVP, 2002), 150.

[4] *Chester Chronicle*, 7 November 2003.

The Teacher: Sheryl Arthur

Sheryl Arthur has a BA in Theology and Religious Studies and an MA in Philosophy and Religion. She has been teaching for five years and is Head of Religious Studies in a girls' grammar school in Surrey. As part of her job she teaches moral issues from a Christian and Muslim perspective at GCSE level and philosophy and ethics at A-level. Sheryl has co-written a textbook and resource pack called *Themes in RE: Learning from Religion*, published by Heinemann.

Challenges

Many still live under the misconception that teaching involves turning up at 9, opening a textbook at the appropriate page for students to take notes or answer comprehension-style questions, leaving at 3.30 and putting your feet up during the generous long holidays. If only it were that simple! Teaching today involves working long hours without paid overtime, teaching a variety of academic subjects, implementing constantly changing government initiatives, justifying results and delivering a programme of Citizenship and Personal, Social and Health Education (PSHE). And for those who are responsible for delivering the Religious Education aspect of the curriculum it provides additional challenges.

In the RE classes in one school that I have experienced (of predominately white, middle-class teenagers) not a week would go by without the whinge of 'What's Hinduism got to do with me? When are we studying our religion?' And when they were asked what 'our religion' might be, the reply was always given in a frustrated way (as though it were a stupid question): 'Christianity – of course.' Yet most of the complainers had barely been near a church, accept for the occasional Christmas carol service, wedding or funeral. When the time finally arrived to study their religion, the whingeing would change to 'What's this got to do with me? I don't want to be a vicar.' Thus the challenge, it would seem, is not only to deliver a lesson that is intellectually stimulating (while incorporating various initiatives such as literacy, numeracy and citizenship), but also, in many schools, to justify to young people (and sometimes other staff) why any form of spiritual learning should be on the timetable at all.

It would seem that we have moved a long way since the 1944 Education Act (sometimes called the Butler Act after the Minister of Education at the time), whereby Religious Instruction, as it was called then, was the only subject that by law had to appear on the state schools' curriculum. In addition, an act of worship (of a Christian nature) would set the tone for the start of each day. Butler himself said, 'It is our hope that our children may seek for themselves in

Christianity, principles which give a purpose to life and a guide to all its problems.'[1]

Indeed, ask anyone born before the 1970s about their experience of religion at school and most will talk about learning the parables and miracles of Jesus or having to sing hymns in the school assembly.

Multifaith approach

There is still some trace of this within the state education system today. However, since the 1988 Education Reform Act, most schools now take a more multifaith approach to Religious Education, requiring students to analyse and evaluate a variety of religious beliefs with tolerance and respect.

The law now states that when teaching religion it is required that it 'shall reflect the fact that the religious traditions in Great Britain are in the main Christian, whilst taking account of the teaching and practices of the other principal religions represented in Great Britain'.[2]

It is understandable that given our multifaith culture and the increasingly harrowing world situation, students do need to be educated in the beliefs of others. Unfortunately, a multifaith curriculum is not without its problems.

In terms of teaching Religious Studies, a very academic subject, there is now much more content to be covered. It is therefore frequently found that pupils muddle the basics of each religion. GCSE mock exam papers tell of Muslims who go to the Bible for guidance or who regularly attend the synagogue. Even though students usually spend five years of secondary school experiencing teaching in six of the major world religions, many leave confused by the many beliefs to choose from and knowing very little of depth about any religion. Hence if they choose to specialise at A-level and beyond, there is much groundwork to be covered before they are able to write at the required standard. It is not rare for 16-year-olds to be unable to name a single miracle of Jesus. Suggestions may vary from 'Didn't he heal someone once?' to references to myths such as 'The Pied Piper of Hamelin'!

It is not just academic knowledge, however, that is affected by the broad curriculum. The multifaith approach is shaping the spiritual development of young people.

Choice

In an increasingly secular society one finds many students viewing belief as a huge choice whereby they can pick and mix the bits that they like from a variety of religions. A commonly held position among students seems to be to accept most of the Christian faith but to ditch Heaven and Hell in favour of the Hindu/Sikh idea of reincarnation. In this day and age the idea that one belief is correct is certainly not politically correct, and so it is swapped for the softer option that you can come back again after death and get a second chance.

Thus it would seem evident that many young people who would call themselves Christians have a very vague understanding of what being a Christian entails. If schools do not introduce young people to faith, it becomes extremely hard for them to access it. Unless a young person has a connection with a church member it is highly unlikely that they will voluntarily enter a church building to seek spiritual fulfilment.

One may naively think that school assemblies successfully initiate a young person into the Christian faith. However, schools need to cater for a multifaith audience, and therefore in many schools, assemblies have simply become a time to reflect on a moral. In many primary schools (those that are not church-affiliated), hymn singing has been replaced by feel-good songs. One student recently recalled to me that in her primary school they used to sing the theme tune of the film *Titanic*; hymns and songs of a Christian nature were prohibited because they offended too many people.

In reality most students can go through eleven years of daily assemblies and still leave with no understanding of the Christian faith.

So maybe we should look to the Religious Studies class to give students the direction they need in terms of spiritual development.

Religious Studies

In 2004 the *Guardian* published a survey claiming that Religious Studies was the fastest-growing A-level course.[3] In one sense this is surprising, since until recently Religious Studies had been attracting very few candidates. Granted, this increase is partially due to the current world situation, and arguably the events of September 11th have sparked off a need to know more about religious belief and practice. Nevertheless, it would also seem that one major attraction is simply growing interest in the subject. But how can this be? Very few students have ever been interested in Religious Education. Maybe it is because many schools no longer offer the traditional option of studying the Old Testament prophets or John's Gospel but instead have started to offer a study of Philosophy of Religion and Ethics, whereby topics such as homosexuality, proofs for the existence of God and life after death are discussed without particular reference to any one religion. Naturally this raises the question: why is philosophy so popular when the theology of the Bible is quite clearly a flop with most young people today?

In discussions with my students they put it down to the fact that they do not want to be presented with one truth claim but want to explore the answers to questions of meaning for themselves, and ultimately to find meaning personally in their lives. They say that this cannot be done if they are presented with one claim to the truth, and that they need to explore many ideas. Although one can well under-stand that to make an informed decision one must have knowledge of more than one truth claim, it is nevertheless worrying that many teenagers today seem to believe there is no point in searching for ultimate truth because there is no objective truth out there to find. They would acquiesce with a philosophical way of thinking called anti-realism: the truth is not something out there to discover, it is not some-thing that one needs to search for, but is something that provides personal meaning for them. It is something that needs to be invented. For example, if you have a place for God in your life then he exists for you; if God has no mean-ing in your life then he does not exist – there is no right and no wrong.

This trend in the thinking of young people in education is obviously characteristic of society as a whole: the view that 'I'll believe what I want, you can believe what you want – as long as that's what makes you happy, that's OK.' However, one cannot help wondering whether the current approach to spirituality in schools has had something to do with shaping these thoughts within young people. Is it possible that presenting so many religions, all claiming to be the 'right way' and also claiming contradictory beliefs, alongside one another may cause students to reject them all, thinking it makes a complete mockery of the whole question of truth? The famous sceptical philosopher Hume made this very point

> All religious systems, it is confessed, are subject to great and insuperable difficulties. Each disputant triumphs in his turn; while he carries on an offensive war, and exposes the absurdities, barbarities, and pernicious tenets of his antagonist. But all of them, on the whole, prepare a complete triumph for the Sceptic; who tells them, that no system ought ever to be embraced with regard to such subjects: For this plain reason, that no absurdity ought ever to be assented to with regard to any subject. A total suspense of judgement is here our only reasonable resource.[4]

Whatever the reason for it, this is an extremely dangerous place to be. It is easy to see why such a philosophy is so attractive. Belief in no objective truth is extremely appealing; it means that one is free to believe whatever one wants, and since one is not claiming to have the Truth, one cannot be criticised. It is politically correct; it tolerates and respects others, and does not offend by conflicting with other truth claims. Therefore the Muslim and the Christian can live peacefully alongside one another since neither claims to have the Truth but merely a truth that provides them personally with meaning in their lives. However, in many respects the attraction ends there. If young people adopt this way of thinking it means that they deny not only the existence of God (objectively) but also any desire to search for the Ultimate Truth. Evangelism therefore becomes an irrelevant issue for any 'Christian' who believes that they are so because Jesus provides their life with personal meaning, since it really does not matter what others believe so long as they are happy.

Not only does this issue affect one's search for truth but it also leads to the denial of absolute moral values, which is an equally distressing topic.

Morality

It is very easy to reflect back in time, or listen to the state of our world as reflected in the news, and feel that moral values are declining; that 'in the good old days' this would never have happened. Whether this is true or not, it is a fact that the United Kingdom has the highest teenage pregnancy rate in Western Europe. In 2002 the under-18 conception rate was 42.6 per thousand females aged 15–17.[5] Fifty-four per cent of all conceptions among under-16-year-olds resulted in a termination in 2000.[6] In 2001–2, in England and Wales, among young people (those aged 16 to 24), thirty-five per cent of men and twenty-four per cent of women said they had taken an illicit drug in the previous year.[7] These statistics alone highlight the huge challenge and responsibility facing those who work in schools with young people today.

One might want to come to the conclusion that the state of morality is due entirely to young people not being initiated into Christian ideals in the home. Admittedly, it's an oversim-plification to say that it is due to lack of Christian guidance. Secularisation, however, may contribute significantly to the problem. Since the nineteenth century Britain has become more and more urbanised. Life for most people (in the cities at least) is based on association. People no longer take owner-ship of the area in which they live, and they tend to know very few people within their neighbourhood personally. It could be argued that since relationships are often impersonal there is no accountability to one another in terms of moral behav-iour. So what does this have to do with secularisation? It is likely that this problem would not arise if people were initiat-ed and brought up in the context of a local church commun-ity. They would have relationship with others within their church family and consequently feel a sense of belonging and identity. This in turn would bring about accountability in terms of moral decisions and their consequences.

So can schools do anything to replace this important aspect of society? While students are in school, obviously it can provide the community and therefore the accountabil-ity. Other than that, it can try to teach morals.

Personal, Social and Health Education (PSHE) has been given a place in the school curriculum for many years, albeit under a variety of guises. According to the Qualifications and Curriculum Authority, it helps to give children and young people the knowledge, skills and understanding they need to lead confident, healthy and independent lives. It endeavours to help them tackle many of the moral, social and cultural issues that are part of growing up. In addition to this, in September 2002 the Government added Citizenship to the school curriculum. Part of the aim of this was to encourage political responsibility. However, these lessons also include issues such as how to be an informed citizen (for example, the need for respect and mutual understanding in terms of religion and ethnic differences) and the importance of resolving conflict fairly and being able to consider other people's experiences or take part responsibly in a school activity.

But does the PSHE and Citizenship curriculum provide students with the moral guidance that they need to function as responsible members of society? Although it can make some contribution, it can never replace the upbringing and accountability that belonging to a faith community provides.

Even if young people do learn morality from formal lessons on their timetable, there is a question we cannot avoid: if we are teaching morality without reference to God, whose values are we instilling? Although many people live a good moral life and reject belief in God, it is hard to define what is right and what is wrong without an agreed reference point. We therefore return to the issue that without an absolute standard to aim for, 'right' and 'wrong' can be whatever you choose to make them.

Right and wrong

When discussing moral issues in schools, students will often have the attitude that an issue is morally wrong for them but they are really not bothered if someone else believes it is morally right. For example, a student recently said to me, 'I believe life begins at conception. Therefore abortion is murder; it is wrong and I could never do it – but it is OK if other people want to do that.' Young people often comment that homosexuality is not right for them but is right for others, or sex before marriage is acceptable to them but they understand if it is not for other people. There does seem to be reluctance among many young people to take a firm stand on any issue and risk being wrong or ridiculed for it. It is much easier, after all, to believe that there is no right or wrong and that one makes one's own values.

So where does this leave us? Should Christians be worried about the lack of biblical knowledge, the growing popularity of the belief that there is no objective truth, the fact that morals are delivered without a Christian framework? How can the message of Christianity be voiced in a multifaith curriculum? Is it possible to run evangelistic activities within the school? Is it permissible to witness within the context of school assemblies?

In one sense, of course, Christians should be concerned. The Bible warns us to 'see to it that no one takes you captive through hollow and deceptive philosophy, which depends on human tradition and the basic principles of this world rather than on Christ' (Col. 2:8). Surely pick-and-mix religion falls under this category, since it seeks popularity through political correctness and a fear of standing up and being counted for something that is extremely unpopular.

The challenge of course is whether or not anything can be done.

Taking a stand

In one sense, while the curriculum is how it is, and while we are living in a society that is multifaith, it is hard to think of any impacting solution.

On the other hand, if Christians are not within the education system there will never be a chance to change or influence the current situation. Christians need to be putting themselves into positions of influence and, when in those positions, ensuring that they are a voice that stands for truth.

In terms of presentation of the Christian faith, if Christians have the calling and indeed privilege of teaching Religious Education within the state system, inevitably they will naturally speak about the Christian faith with conviction and compassion. It is not acceptable, however, for teachers to indoctrinate or misuse their influence and position of authority when often dealing with vulnerable minds. After all, if Christianity is the Ultimate Truth, if presented to young people fairly it is quite capable of standing up for itself academically when put alongside other belief systems.

Most schools do allow a Christian Union to meet, and while it may not be possible to actively evangelise outside the meeting, it is possible to provide support and encouragement for those who are already Christians or for those who voluntarily want to explore the faith further. This in turn has a mushrooming effect. Christian students who are secure in their beliefs stand up for truth, and thereby witness to others.

Ultimately through prayer Christians need to be taking a stand. Christians, both within the education system and outside it, need to be praying not only for young people but also for the teachers, head teachers and policymakers who strive to make a difference in an increasingly challenging profession.

1 Cited by M. Grimmitt in 'Evolving Styles of Religious Education in England', *Word in Life*, August 1981, 137.
2 Education Act 1988, section 8.
3 *Guardian*, 19 August 2004.
4 Hume, David, *Dialogues Concerning Natural Religion*, part 2, 1779.
5 *Opportunity for all*, Department of Work and Pensions report, 2004.
6 National Statistics Online.
7 National Statistics Online.

The Political Observer: Don Horrocks

Don Horrocks is Head of Public Affairs at the Evangelical Alliance. He previously spent twenty-five years in corporate banking and management consultancy. Don completed his doctorate at the London School of Theology in 2001 and has published a book on the development of soteriological thought in the nineteenth century. He has headed the EA's Policy Commission for six years, editing books on Transsexuality and GM crops and foods as well as contributing to publications on theology and social ethics. Don is married with three children, and enjoys mountain walking.

Under threat

The church today is operating in a new environment. The rise of liberal secular democracy, with its pluralist attitude to religion, its insistence on strict religious neutrality and tolerance, its humanistic hostility to anything apart from privatised faith and its unquestioning assumption of the supremacy of individual human rights, is subtly undermining practices that have previously been taken for granted. No longer can we rely on the state to actively encourage, still less to fund, distinctively Christian mission. Despite the state's superficially benign attitude, its backing for challenges to the church both in Europe and the UK suggests that the preaching of the Gospel as we know it could be under threat.

The threat is subtle because it comes disguised as a desire to preserve religious liberty and extend religious rights. Secularism and pluralism combine, however, to produce a lowest common denominator form of religion. We see its fruits springing up everywhere. Where once government or public bodies and Christian groups would regularly interact on matters of public policy, suddenly the latter are being expected to submit to interfaith forums, endorse faith-based initiatives, and bow to human rights supremos. The distinctive Christian voice has become one among many and can be outvoted if perceived to be out of line with a politically correct agenda. Christians are nowadays bad news, as events in 2004 during the nomination of Roman Catholic Rocco Buttiglione to the European Commission demonstrated only too clearly. The champions of tolerance become intolerant when they encounter religious conviction in the public arena. And they are blind to any inconsistency in their overtly discriminatory approach.

Christian groups are already experiencing discriminatory treatment. For example, in universities, in the area of Christian broadcasting and in the sphere of local government funding, they increasingly encounter pressure from state authorities with politically correct agendas to water down a specifically Christian ethos or motivation, or indeed to dispense with it altogether. Measures which tend to undermine marriage and family are worrying trends that directly affect the Christian world, and those who seek to protect traditional values frequently meet with open hostility. There are fears that fundamental, inalienable religious freedoms hitherto preserved in the European Declaration of Human Rights, such as liberty to preach the Gospel and freedom of association, may become subordinate to individual rights. A new hierarchy of rights is emerging as a result of interpretations by the courts, where judicial activism akin to that seen in the USA is becoming a worrying feature.

Political agendas

In recent times Christian groups such as the Evangelical Alliance have found themselves engaging with, critiquing or opposing proposed government legislation which they see as potentially threatening to basic Christian freedoms. They have traditionally concentrated on seeking to influence the democratic political processes, but it has become increasingly necessary to widen the scope of political monitoring to include the courts, and even to become directly involved in strategically important legal cases. Christians more and more find themselves having to work within a UK and European public framework characterised by the following:

- A tendency for Parliament to pass laws which deal with ambiguous general principles, leaving interpretation and detailed outworking in the hands of the courts.

- Increasing recourse to the courts rather than Parliament to determine conflict issues, especially those involving human rights and discrimination.
- The proliferation of European directives and guidelines bearing unavoidable future implications for UK law and the Christian/faith constituencies.
- The emergence of a single human rights and equality body incorporating a 'religion' strand as one among several subsumed within an overall secular framework and ethos.
- The awareness of potential co-belligerent strategic partners who share Christian concerns but operate out of wholly distinct perspectives.
- The increasing likelihood of churches, individuals and organisations facing legal restrictions or legal actions, even potentially leading to imprisonment. Such actions may well be politically or maliciously orchestrated. Access to legal advice may be lacking and/or fighting funds may not be readily available.

Churches and Christian organisations are increasingly falling foul of secularist 'politically correct' agendas that aim to attack and undermine religious liberty and freedom of conscience. The catalogue of recent liberty issues affecting Christians includes:

- New employment regulations outlawing religious and sexual orientation discrimination.
- Gender recognition of transsexual people (where churches' ability to regulate themselves may be undermined).
- Sunday working.

- Clergy employment rights.
- Discrimination issues, including public funding of faith-based organisations.
- The teaching of religion in publicly funded schools.
- The wearing of religious symbols.
- The holding of religious meetings in publicly funded institutions.
- The creation of 'sect' law.
- Freedom to preach the Gospel.
- Freedom for university Christian Unions to require appointed officers to subscribe to a basis of faith.
- Questioning of the inalienable nature of religious liberties enshrined in the European Convention on Human Rights.
- Charitable 'public benefit' criteria.
- Marriage, family and right-to-life issues.

We will now look at two recent or proposed pieces of crucial legislation that are seen as likely to impact the life and mission of the local church and Christian organisations.

1. Equality and diversity: the employment regulations

Some Christian groups, including the Evangelical Alliance, picked up the Employment Regulations legislation on their early warning systems several years before it was introduced in the UK Parliament. The origin of these regulations was Article 13 of the Treaty of Amsterdam, in fulfilment of which the European Union institutions produced two directives. One of them, the Employment Directive, prohibited discrimination in employment on the grounds of age, disability, sexual orientation, religion or belief. Member states were required to incorporate it into their domestic law by December 2003.[1]

The human rights that most concern politicians tend to be those of individuals. Religion, however, is not an exclusively individualistic matter. In most religions, believers associate in faith-based organisations for worship, instruction, mission and other activities. To ignore this in the implementation of the anti-discrimination legislation could in practice have led to more religious discrimination, not less. That would be the result if religious organisations were not allowed to recruit from their own faith communities in order to preserve their distinctive religious ethos, traditions and identities.

Occupational requirement

So the Employment Directive allowed religious organisations to practise a 'difference of treatment' in relation to posts for which religion or belief 'constitutes a genuine, legitimate and justified occupational requirement'. Religious organisations were also given the right 'to require individuals working for them to act in good faith and with loyalty to the organisation's ethos'. However, this did not give employers carte blanche to discriminate. In a world where equal treatment is considered of paramount importance, difference of treatment has to be justified – if that is possible. In relation to posts involving leadership, policy making, representation and instruction in the faith it could be expected that this should not prove difficult. In relation to posts requiring technical or manual skills, for example in the case of a caretaker, a secretary, a cook or a bookkeeper, it might be difficult in practice to insist that appointees must also belong to the faith.

The regulations were the result of a lengthy consultation process. A major issue in the consultation was the perceived fault line running through the first draft of the legislation between the religion and sexual orientation provisions. Some religious organisations wanted to distinguish between sexual orientation and practice and to retain the right not to employ people engaging in sexual activities incompatible with the teaching of the Scriptures. Gay and secularist lobby groups saw this as discrimination and sought to prevent it.

For the most part, the religion regulations laid before Parliament in May 2003 closely followed the European directive. The right to require an employee to act in good faith and with loyalty to the organisation was in any case already implied in existing employment law in the form of a contract of employment involving a duty of trust and confidence on the part of both employer and employee. An employee acting in bad faith or without loyalty to the employer's ethos would be in breach of this duty and could be dismissed.

Even more significant was the inclusion in the final draft of the sexual orientation regulations of a provision allowing religious organisations to apply a requirement related to sexual orientation that complies with their doctrines.

Ethos

The regulations were seen as permitting religious organisations a measure of freedom to recruit selectively from their faith community in order to preserve their religious ethos – with two qualifications. First, such freedom presupposed that these organisations actually have an ethos that reflects what they purport to believe. And second, that the requirement for a Christian specifically to fill a particular post could be demonstrably justified as a 'genuine occupational requirement'. Parliament did not decide, and it was immediately anticipated that case law would be needed to reveal how far such freedom could be stretched. Of course, many religious organisations were only too well aware that it would be unwise to expect employment tribunals to have any well-developed understanding of religious organisations and what might be an appropriate ethos for them to have.

The exceptional treatment of religion and belief was inevitably unpopular with secular humanists and others with self-interest or anti-religious agendas. The wisdom and sensitivity with which the religion provisions were applied in practice would be crucial in determining how well they worked and how long they survived pressures to remove them. It was evident straightaway that if religious organisations sought to apply a 'genuine occupational requirement' to every post in order to exclude unbelievers at all costs, they would inevitably be in breach of the regulations and find themselves taken to a tribunal. Smaller organisations in which every employee could significantly influence the ethos and all employees interacted with the public might find it easier to justify such a policy than larger ones. In that sense, the legislation was seen as potentially impinging on the religious liberty of larger faith-based organisations. The modest concessions obtained in the regulations were undoubtedly due in large part to the successful lobbying activity of Christian groups like the Evangelical Alliance from the earliest stages of the draft directive in Brussels to the introduction of the regulations by the UK Government.

Judicial review

Few people imagined how quickly the new regulations would be challenged by those who objected to their perceived discriminatory aspects. The Government's interpretation of the European directive was almost immediately put to the test. In December 2003, the Employment Equality (Sexual Orientation) Regulations 2003 came into force. Almost immediately seven trade unions brought a claim for judicial review against the Secretary of State for Trade and Industry on the grounds that the scope of certain provisions was unlawfully discriminatory. The case was heard in the High Court on 17–19 March 2004.[2] Three key regulations were challenged:

- The regulation which permits employers (whether secular or faith-based) in certain circumstances to discriminate lawfully in relation to specific posts on the grounds of an individual's sexual orientation or practice.
- The regulation which permits employers (where the employment is for the purposes of an organised religion) in certain circumstances to discriminate lawfully on the grounds of an individual's sexual orientation or practice.
- The regulation which excludes the provision of benefits dependent on marital status from the scope of the regulations.

Three Christian organisations (the Evangelical Alliance, CARE and the Christian Schools Trust) took the bold step of intervening in the proceedings to ensure that the views of Christians were heard by the High Court. Certain of these groups had been monitoring the introduction of the regulations from their genesis several years earlier as a draft European directive in the European Commission (where they had successfully lobbied for the interests of religious groups to be taken on board) right up to their debate in Parliament only months before the judicial review. The three Christian organisations were obliged to underwrite the potential costs of challenging the review – by no means a risk-free step.

High Court decision

The Christian partners were to a significant degree successful. When Mr Justice Richards delivered the High Court judgement on 26 April 2004 he dismissed the unions' claims. The Court upheld historic understandings that same-sex partners were not in a comparable position to married couples and could therefore be treated differently. Furthermore, the Court accepted that the rights of Christians were engaged under the Human Rights Act 1998 and there was consequently a need to take their interests into account when applying the regulations.

The Court held, however, that the exemptions under the regulations applying to lawful discrimination in respect of sexual orientation and practice were to be 'given a narrow construction' and were to be 'construed strictly . . . and purposively . . . [allowing] an exception only in very limited circumstances'. In particular, the Court held that in relation to the requirement 'so as to comply with the doctrines of the religion', it would be necessary to demonstrate convincingly that employment of a person not meeting the requirement would be incompatible with the doctrines of the religion. According to the Court, the scope for doing that is 'very narrow'. Similar comments were made in relation to the alternative requirement ('because of the nature of the employment and the context in which it is carried out, so as to avoid conflicting with the strongly held religious convictions of a significant number of the religion's followers'). This too would need to be tested objectively and in the view of the Court, in practice it would most likely be 'a very far from easy test to satisfy in practice'. The Court considered it 'inappropriate' to state in which circumstances the provisions could be relied upon successfully, significantly leaving it open for future cases to be decided on their own facts.

Implications for Christian organisations

While the freedom of Christian organisations to employ those who subscribe to Christian ethos and belief has been largely preserved, that freedom has become somewhat constrained and the law in some areas remains ambiguous until tested in the courts. It is likely that many Christian organisations that may be seeking to rely upon the exemptions contained in the regulations will not be able to do so as a result of the High Court's decision. For example, the Court stated that the employment of a teacher at a faith-based school is likely to be 'for purposes of a religious organisation' but not 'for purposes of an organised religion'. That being so, the school would have to show that being of a particular sexual orientation was a genuine and determining occupational requirement for that particular teaching post before it could lawfully discriminate on the grounds of sexual orientation. In practice this could be extremely difficult. For example, advertisements for secretarial jobs with Christian employers which state 'commitment to the evangelical Christian faith' as a necessary requirement are likely to be rejected as both direct religious discrimination and indirect discrimination by potentially disqualifying applicants of a particular sexual orientation – unless it can be clearly demonstrated that being an evangelical Christian is a 'genuine occupational requirement' for a particular job.

So despite apparent victory in the High Court, Christian employers have actually had freedoms taken away from them as a result of the regulations. But it took a great deal of strategic analysis and planning, political and legal expertise, courage and determination, and not least risk, on the part of the interveners to achieve a measure of protection for Christians to continue legally to uphold their beliefs and practices in the field of employment. It is clear, however, that the debate is not over yet; although the appellants decided not to appeal the judgement, it will be actual future cases that determine how the law will evolve. This makes it almost inevitable that sooner or later Christian employers will have little choice but to defend themselves in Court if they wish to preserve their autonomy.

2. Proposals to repeal the laws of blasphemy and introduce a new law outlawing religious hatred

In July 2004 the Home Secretary announced the introduction of a new law to protect faith groups from religious hatred. The Government has been motivated by a wish to deter those who seek to stir up hatred against religious groups, especially Muslims, an issue which has become more pressing following the September 11th terrorist attack in New York. It seems determined to plug the gap whereby Muslims (as a non-racial group) are not specifically protected. Christians would also gain protection – but unlike the Muslims they have not sought such protection. There are also concurrent plans to repeal the laws on blasphemy and outlaw religious discrimination, sex discrimination and sexual orientation discrimination in relation to goods and services. This would extend the law relating to discriminatory treatment from employment to catch virtually every area of public life – including churches. As proved to be the case during the debate over the Gender Recognition Bill in the 2003/4 session of Parliament, as far as churches are concerned, the fundamental issues related not so much to transsexualism as such, but to the right of churches to regulate their own affairs in accordance with their beliefs.

Religious freedoms

While Christians unequivocally support measures that would effectively prevent incitement to hatred, it is equally imperative to preserve religious freedoms and beliefs and the right to express them. And it is not just religious freedoms that are at stake. There are basic civil liberties relating to freedom of speech which need to be defended.[3]

Unless the Government listens carefully to the concerns of Christian groups and others, there is a real danger that the rights and freedoms they have always enjoyed may suffer in the future as a result of the courts' interpretation of Parliament's intentions. Under such measures it is possible that in the future a Christian could, for example, be prosecuted for criticising someone else's beliefs, or for asserting the exclusive claims of Jesus. Historic Christianity insists on the uniqueness and divinity of Jesus Christ and this belief can never be compromised for Christians. Similarly, Christian broadcasters may find themselves censured for quoting the Bible. Mission organisations may be monitored for the claims made in their literature. Even the editor of *Muslim News* has expressed concern over potential prosecution for offending Christians by denying the claims of Christ.

It is not that special privileges are sought for Christians. But what is needed is a clear and effective commitment by Parliament to maintain religious freedom for all when it legislates. Not only that, but specific affirmations are essential, guaranteeing that Christians, Muslims, Hindus and members of any other faith group will be allowed to observe the rites, doctrines and traditions of their beliefs, and be permitted to continue to express them openly without fear of prosecution.

Religious hatred

The Government proposes to achieve its objectives by making it a criminal offence to incite religious hatred. Legislation would most likely extend existing law contained in the Public Order Act 1986 and the Crime and Disorder Act 1998, which presently covers offences involving racial hatred, to include religious hatred. The Government has stated that it does not intend to restrict the longstanding tradition of rights to freedom of speech in Britain, and people will remain free to criticise religion or religious practices. Its stated aim is to preserve the right to practise one's own religion without fear of assault, and it believes that there is a difference (which can be reflected in legal terms) between criticising a religion and inciting hatred through a criminal act. What is at issue is whether or not the Government can achieve its objective without undermining civil liberties.

Based on what the Government sought to do in 2001, it is anticipated that an individual will be in breach of the proposed legislation if they use threatening, abusive or insulting words or behaviour intended or likely to stir up hatred against a group of people because of their religious belief.

It remains unclear how the Government will distinguish in practice between intentional and unintentional stirring up of hatred, between the likelihood and unlikelihood of hatred being stirred up. Unlike in issues of race, we are dealing here with subjective categories of belief and opinion, so it may in practice be extremely difficult to differentiate between intention to offend and the taking of offence, or to gauge the subjective dimension of likelihood where variable tolerance thresholds have to be taken into account. Though the Government insists that a high threshold of tolerance will be built into the legislation, it is difficult to see how this would actually work, especially as different religious groups may exhibit widely differing levels of tolerance of criticism of their faith.

The proposed religious hatred legislation is expected to cover hatred directed against others who have no faith and also hatred against a group who do not share the particular religious beliefs of another group or individual.

Blasphemy

Assurances have been given that the Attorney General will identify cases deemed to be trivial or vindictive, and there is evidence from Scotland and Northern Ireland (where religious hatred law already exists) that only the most serious of cases are actually taken forward to prosecution. Nevertheless, Christians need to remain on the alert and be prepared to engage with the political processes at every level to make their views known. The intentions that underlie the proposed legislation are to be commended. All faith groups should welcome proposals designed to protect them from incitement to hatred. Christians and others, however, need to emphasise their concerns about the perceived threat to religious liberties, and especially the freedom to express their faith and oppose views they believe to be untrue, without fear of prosecution.

With regard to blasphemy, while many Christians and members of other faiths welcome a new offence of religious hatred in principle (provided that civil liberties are preserved), they believe that the existing blasphemy laws, though rarely used nowadays, should be retained for their symbolic value rather than abolished or extended. It would send out the wrong signal to society that blasphemy is an outdated concept and that the values the existing law enshrines are not worth keeping. Though privileging the

Church of England, the blasphemy laws are still seen as exercising a restraining umbrella protective force for all faiths. And there is still a qualitative distinction between blasphemy and religious hatred.

Prophetic voice

If our culture has lost its Judaeo-Christian moral and ethical base, which has stood society in good stead for so long, the role of evangelical Christians needs to become essentially a prophetic one. Through professional and academic highlighting of the evidence demonstrating what is happening to society, the prophetic task includes speaking out firmly but with compassion and persuading those who occupy the public forum of how such trends are harmful to society.

However, this does not stop Christians pointing out what God has to say. Popular caricatures of evangelical Christians often portray them as all censoriousness and clamour, supposedly always taken up with moral campaigns. In fact, it is more accurate to say that most active evangelicals devote their energies to issues of social justice and liberty – traditional preoccupations of evangelicals. After all, human rights are rooted in the Judaeo-Christian tradition and evangelicals reject accusations that such a worldview is outdated, irrelevant and redundant. They rightly make no apology for adopting the perspective of countless millions of people around the world who think it makes good sense for people to follow their Maker's instructions. Of course, Christians can't and don't want to impose their views on society. Nevertheless, they have a perfectly valid concern to avoid erosion of what they believe to be the common good. Since they argue that virtue and happiness belong together, doesn't it make sense to promote virtue? This affords a perfectly legitimate basis for applying a Christian worldview to particularly controversial moral issues such as human sexuality. Again, the prophetic role of the church is to challenge the accepted view and where necessary say it's wrong. But we cannot impose such views on society.

Of course, at the same time it is true that society cannot impose its values and worldview on the church. This is a basic human right of religious liberty and any attempt to undermine and erode the church's worldview ultimately must be resisted. It's something Christians must be prepared to die for!

------

[1] This section is based on an article which first appeared in the Evangelical Alliance's publication *PQ* in May 2003.

[2] This section is based on an article which first appeared in the Evangelical Alliance's publication *PQ* in May 2004, reported by Peng Voong and Andrea Minichiello Williams of the Lawyers' Christian Fellowship.

[3] This section is based partly on briefing material produced jointly by the Evangelical Alliance and CARE for the Anti-Terrorism, Crime and Security Bill in 2001. Following lobbying by Christian groups and others the religious hatred aspects of the Bill were dropped.

5

The University Chaplains: Jenny Dyer and Mark Bratton

Revd Mark Bratton was a barrister and Revd Jenny Dyer a solicitor before they entered the ministry. Mark Bratton specialised in medical law and ethics. He has been Anglican chaplain at Warwick University for six years and Area Dean of Coventry South for three years. Jenny Dyer specialised in charity law. She has been Free Church chaplain at Warwick for three years, and is also minister of three churches in the Coventry Methodist Circuit. Each is married with two children.

Warwick University – a case study

Baiting the Christian Union (CU) is a traditional and popular blood sport in Students' Unions. Many university CUs have a lengthy cyclical history of affiliation and disaffiliation, usually depending on the presence or absence of a sympathetic team of Union sabbatical officers. The CU often rises to the bait, choosing to eschew the privileges of Union membership with some melodramatic gesture of Christian distinctiveness and remembering that the persecuted are blessed. And then, perhaps to the chagrin of the university chaplain, it decamps to the chaplaincy, where alternative resources – such as meeting space, photocopying and minibus hire – can be found.

In the 2003/4 academic year, a motion was put to the University College London (UCL) Students' Union (SU) to dis-affiliate the Christian Union because of its affiliation to the Universities and Colleges Christian Fellowship (UCCF). The motion, which was on this occasion voted down by a con-siderable margin, was directed at all religious societies and asserted that they were by nature sectarian and therefore unconstitutional. At about the same time, the Hull University Students' Union was refusing to ratify the Christian Union's revised constitution, which required a firm Christian com-mitment of all its Executive members and a written endorse-ment of the UCCF Doctrinal Basis. This requirement was said to be in breach of the Union's Equal Opportunities policy because it ruled out in principle the possibility of the Christian Union being run by non-Christians.

Sexuality

A number of the spats over the last ten years have con-cerned Christian views on homosexuality. In Leeds the Students' Union threatened to debar the CU from using SU rooms for meetings unless it agreed not to quote from Romans 1. Leicester SU came close to breaking a contract with a group of local churches which had hired SU rooms for a gathering, again over the sexuality issue. In York, the CU was accused of 'homophobia' when two of its members ran an Alpha course in SU-controlled rooms. At Warwick, the CU was disaffiliated from the SU for giving advice that same-sex sex is a sin.

The events at Warwick University which led to the CU's disaffiliation began in March 2002. The CU President received an email from someone he did not know, who said that he was worried about feelings he was having for other men. There is some suspicion, in the light of what happened subsequently, that this was not a genuine request, and that the name used was a pseudonym. A search revealed nobody of that name on the university's email network.

The CU President at first said that he did not feel qualified to help, and offered to refer the inquirer to a particular pastor. The inquirer persisted in asking for advice, however, so the CU President gave some, in the form of an email attachment two-and-a-half pages long.

The tone of the advice was sympathetic, though the views expressed were definitely conservative evangelical. The CU President began by drawing a distinction between intense male friendship and homosexuality. Then, because he was uncertain about the inquirer's religious background, he customised his advice according to whether the inquirer was a Christian or not.

On the assumption that the inquirer was a Christian, he offered a series of biblical texts which in his view demonstrated that homosexual practice is wrong, and more generally that any 'sexuality' that deviates from the divine (heterosexual) blueprint is a distortion of the divine image in us and a symptom of human fallenness. He then exhorted the inquirer in general terms to struggle against sinful tendencies (and clearly homosexual tendencies were intended to be included among them). He also offered practical advice: a call to prayer in the assurance of God's forgiveness for sins; to put oneself out of temptation's way; to get involved in a local church and/or the Christian Union.

Then, on the assumption that the inquirer was not a Christian, he offered a more generalised statement about the universality of human sin and the imperative to repent and receive the Gospel, leading to the possibility of a Spirit-filled life.

In his reply, the inquirer expressed himself to be grateful for the time and attention given.

Complaint

The advice document very quickly found its way into the hands of the Lesbian, Gay, Bisexual and Transsexual (LGBT) Campaign Convenor – an ex-student with a semi-official role at the Students' Union to advise and campaign on LGBT issues. Through him, it found its way to the student newspaper, the *Warwick Boar*. The *Boar* printed an editorial in April entitled 'Christian Union in "homophobic" row', which insinuated that the CU might find itself in breach of the Students' Union's Welfare and Equal Opportunities policy on two grounds: firstly, the exclusion of homosexual members from membership, and secondly, the failure to provide 'an environment free from intimidation or victimisation on any grounds including ... sexual orientation'.

From the article, it appeared that the CU President had said, when challenged by the *Boar*, that a person's homosexuality would diminish their chances of receiving his personal vote if they stood for election to the CU Exec. He had subsequently tried to withdraw this remark before the article was printed.

The LGBT Campaign Convenor made a disciplinary complaint against the Christian Union to the Students' Union, and in May the Students' Union informed the CU of its decision to take the matter to a disciplinary hearing. The charge was twofold:

- discrimination based on sexual orientation.
- not providing a safe and welcoming environment for LGBT students who may wish to join the Christian Union.

We, the Anglican and Free Church chaplains, submitted a document and attended the hearing in support of the CU. We did not do this to support a particular stance on homosexuality, but because we felt that the CU was in danger of being treated unjustly. It seemed to us that on this occasion it was not LGBT students who were being harassed and victimised, as claimed, but the CU.

We were concerned to make a number of points. Firstly, we were concerned about the rather general and unspecific nature of the allegations on the 'charge sheet'. The CU should know what case it had to answer. The reference to LGBT students who may wish to join the CU was purely speculative.

Secondly, we wanted to make the point that there is probably a wider range of views on homosexuality within the CU than in some of the other faith societies on campus. Warwick is a highly international community, with twenty to twenty-five per cent international students, and among the Students' Union societies there are a large Islamic Society, a Jewish-Israeli Society, and societies for Hindus, Jains, Sikhs, Buddhists and Bahais. Clearly, it would not have been politically correct for the LGBT Convenor to take action against these. The CU provided an easy target.

Thirdly, we pointed out that the advice given had been solicited, indeed pestered for, by the inquirer. The CU President had spent considerable time and thought putting it together, and it evinced care and concern and a complete absence of hostility. Was that really unwelcoming? The charge that an LGBT student would not be safe in a CU meeting was entirely without foundation. He or she might not like some of the views they heard expressed, but then an Islamic student might not like all that he heard in a meeting of the Jewish-Israeli Society, nor a Zionist all that she heard in the Islamic Society.

Hearing

The hearing took place on 27 May 2002. The disciplinary panel looked at the advice given by the CU President to the inquirer. It also considered the content on the CU's website in relation to homosexuality, and a link on the CU website to the True Freedom Trust, an organisation that claims it can help counsel gay people out of their homosexuality.

In fact, the Christian Union survived the hearing pretty much unscathed. The panel of Students' Union officers who heard the case seemed to have a fair amount of sympathy for them. The CU representatives were contrite, apologising if they had offended anybody. The alleged inquirer was not present, and neither was the LGBT Convenor.

The panel stopped short of finding the CU in breach of the Union's Equal Opportunities policy, but held that they were guilty of having 'made mistakes'. The penalties they imposed were fairly minor. In particular, the CU had to send an email to the person who had originally sought the advice, describing the variety of Christian views on the subject of homosexuality, and they had to remove the offending link to the True Freedom Trust from their website. The panel expressed some concern that the CU may have been the victim of an entrapment and, without saying whether they thought this was the case, decided to take steps to make it impossible in the future for disciplinary complaints to be brought by way of an entrapment.

The panel made it clear that if in future the CU were approached with another such request, they were not at liberty to say, 'This is what we believe.' They must instead give a balanced answer, saying, 'Some Christians believe this, but then other Christians believe that.' As chaplains, we were intrigued by this. Presumably this would also be the Students' Union's view on how we as chaplains should respond to similar inquiries. Of course, the Students' Union's writ does not run as far as the chaplaincy, but we are nevertheless subject to the university's Equal Opportunities policy.

Disaffiliation

Warwick Pride (the society for LGBT students) was deeply unhappy with the panel's findings. There was at the time no mechanism for an appeal seeking that the sanctions be increased. Warwick Pride therefore threatened instead to table a motion for the Union Council seeking the temporary disaffiliation of the CU, unless it agreed to certain terms. It had to apologise for its behaviour, remove its support for the

True Freedom Trust, refer on to approved counsellors any-one mooting personal issues relating to homosexuality, and actively encourage LGBT students to play a full part in the CU.

Warwick Pride was predictably unhappy with the CU's less than total acceptance of these terms, and so the motion was duly tabled. In an email to the CU, its President said, 'We have taken this action, as you know, to protect LGBT students at Warwick from the "advice" and information that you have been giving over the last few weeks. . . . I regret having to take this action, but you have left us with little choice.'

The Union Council Meeting took place on 20 June. It was somewhat less good-natured than the disciplinary hearing had been. There was much hostility from those proposing the motion. The CU were grovelling, even craven, in their eagerness to demonstrate good faith and Christian humility. Their rep said, as quoted in the minutes, '. . . we have apologised for anything we have done which has caused offence to any individual or group. We are working with the recommendations from the Disciplinary Hearing, we are sorry for the mistakes we may have made, we wish to work with the Officers, to move on.'

Initially the meeting was inquorate, a fairly routine problem. This was overcome in an ingenious way. An emergency motion was tabled proposing a change to the election regulations. It stipulated, retrospectively from the beginning of that academic year, that all Union Council members who had missed four meetings without sending apologies would be deemed to have resigned from the Council. This was passed, rendering the Council Meeting quorate. The Council then resolved to disaffiliate the CU for a year, this decision to be reviewed at a subsequent meeting. The *Warwick Boar* reported the CU's expulsion in somewhat extravagant terms under the headline, 'CU thrown to the lions', and a short paragraph or two about it appeared in some of the broadsheets.

Disaffiliation does not mean that the CU cannot exist, but only that it is no longer a Students' Union society. The main practical effect for the CU was that they were no longer able to hold their main meetings in the 'Cooler' in the Students' Union building. Instead, they now have these in a large lecture theatre, the chaplaincy not being big enough. Many smaller CU events are held in the chaplaincy. The CU was also not able to have flyers printed and distributed free of charge to all freshers at the beginning of the next academic year. Instead, they themselves printed some tiny flyers (half A5 size, to save money) and we distributed these inside chaplaincy leaflets, along with (bigger) flyers for the other (smaller) Christian societies. This was a bit of a comedown for them. They were also unable to have a stall at the Freshers' Fayre. They were allowed to set up a table outside the door of the building in which the Fayre was held, and this arguably worked to their advantage, giving them greater prominence. Nevertheless, it was noticeable that Christian Focus, the chaplaincy-based, more liberal Christian society, had a higher membership than usual in the next academic year, probably at the CU's expense.

Fallout

The situation has remained unchanged since June 2002. The Christian Union has not subsequently sought reaffiliation to the Students' Union. On 16 October 2002, the Union Council considered the matter further, and resolved in strong language, 'to condemn the views previously expressed by the Christian Union with regard to homosexuality', and to allow a reaffiliation only if the CU can 'prove to be fully upholding of the Students' Union Equal Opportunities policy'.

There was some limited fallout in the chaplaincy. Some liberal Christian students informed the chaplains that we were now branded a 'homophobic' chaplaincy nationally for having supported the CU. We were assured by liberal Christians that the CU's views were 'illegal', and this seemed to be widely believed. Both of us having been lawyers before we entered the ministry, we tried to explain that they were not illegal, in the sense of constituting an offence, though they might be considered 'unlawful' in a lesser sense, if they were found to contravene an Equal Opportunities policy. It concerned us, in a university of all places, to find people who refused to engage in debate on a matter, simply ruling the other side of the argument illegitimate. On the sexuality question, it is usually those on the conservative side of the debate who take this line; in this case it was those on the liberal side. Political correctness ruled.

Subsequently, a motion was brought to the Union Council censuring the chaplaincy for allowing the CU to use chaplaincy facilities, but this was lost. Even if passed, it would simply have been the opinion of the Students' Union and would have had no practical effect.

The disaffiliation was of course an internal Students' Union matter, and the Union has authority to regulate its own affairs. However, British universities have responsibilities under the education legislation to ensure that the Students' Union does not breach legislation or behave in clear conflict with university disciplinary and other codes.

The Registrar took a look at what had happened and came to the view that the Students' Union was not acting in suppression of free speech, and that it had not broken any disciplinary code, so he took no action.

Law

The university's Equal Opportunities policy states that it 'aims to eliminate discrimination on grounds of gender, race, nationality, ethnic or national origin, political beliefs, religious beliefs or practices, disability, marital status, family circumstances, sexual orientation, spent criminal convictions, age or any other appropriate ground'. The Students' Union's policy is framed in similar terms.

There is therefore a commitment to eliminate discrimination on the grounds of sexual orientation, but also a commitment to outlaw discrimination on the grounds of religious belief. Arguably, in a situation like that which arose at Warwick, neither of these is absolute, but each needs to be balanced against the other. Furthermore, British universities are legally obliged to ensure that they operate in a fair, democratic and accountable manner, and to guarantee freedom of speech on campus. Section 43(1) of the Education (No.2) Act 1986 states

> Every individual and body of persons concerned in the government of any establishment to which this section applies shall take such steps as are reasonably practicable to ensure that freedom of speech within the law is secured for members, students and employees of the establishment and for visiting speakers.

Moreover, subsection (2) provides

> The duty imposed by subsection (1) above includes (in particular) the duty to ensure, so far as is reasonably practicable, that the use of any premises of the establishment is not denied to any individual or body of persons on any ground connected with –
>
> (a) The beliefs or views of that individual or of any member of that body ...

Again, rights to freedom of speech and religion are not absolute. A framework for balancing the conflicting rights is given by Article 9 of the European Convention on Human Rights (which relates to freedom of thought, conscience and religion). This was incorporated into domestic law through the Human Rights Act 1998, and provides in Schedule 1, Part I, Article 9

> Freedom to manifest one's religion or beliefs shall be subject only to such limitations as are prescribed by law and are necessary in a democratic society in the interests of public safety, for the protection of public order, health or morals, or for the protection of the rights and freedoms of others.

Similar qualifications apply to the right to freedom of expression.

Freedom

The difficulty here is whether or not the mere expression, by an individual or a group, of a socially conservative attitude towards homosexual practice is by definition unacceptable, in that it automatically threatens the rights and freedoms of gay people. This view is intelligible if we place these attitudes in the same category as racist and sexist views. But if they are seen as part of the legitimate diversity of opinion on the subject within society, then perhaps a distinction could be drawn between mere expressions of opinion and actual condemnatory action. Within the Students' Union culture at Warwick, it is clear that the first of these approaches is taken: 'homophobic' opinion is seen as wholly unacceptable, like racist or sexist views, and not as within a legitimate spectrum of views. If the Students' Union is indicative of how society will be in the future, then maybe society is moving that way too.

There is a perception among evangelical Christians that they are being singled out as uniquely culpable, even though similarly conservative views on the issue of homosexual practice are held and expressed by members of many of the other religious groups, whose affiliation to the Students' Union is unchallenged. One Warwick student describes how a gay friend was taken to task in a university café for wearing a T-shirt emblazoned with a cross. Had he been similarly reprimanded as a Jew for wearing a Star of David or as a Muslim for sporting the crescent moon, it would surely have become a disciplinary matter.

6

The Barrister: Paul Diamond

Paul Diamond is a barrister practising in public, employment and housing law. He also specialises in the law of religious liberty. He was called to the Bar in 1985 and was barrister to the *Keep Sunday Special* campaign. In 1997 he took the banning of a Pro-Life Alliance party election broadcast to the European Court. In recent years he has argued a number of ground-breaking cases on religious and education rights. From 1991 to 1995 he served as a councillor on Cambridge City Council. Paul is married, with two sons.

An extraordinary tale

Let me tell you a story about a far-off country. The names of the people and places involved have been changed to preserve anonymity. The story involves a brave British missionary in a non-Christian country. I shall refer to him as Mr H.

Mr H was an evangelical preacher of the quintessential British eccentric variety. I use the term 'was', as he is now dead. In the final years of his life, Mr H suddenly found himself in the public eye when he became the subject of a court case. He was 68 years old at the time of his purported offence, and prior to this date he had been regarded as a man of good character. What happened to him was unpleasant, but sadly it was not an isolated incident; indeed, it was a reflection of the current state of affairs in this distant country.

Mr H used to preach regularly in the town of B, a seaside resort on the south coast of this land. One day, he went down to the central square and preached on the subject of homosexuality. He declared to the citizens of the town that this kind of sexual activity was contrary to God's word. To make matters worse, he carried a banner that read, 'Stop immorality, stop homosexuality, stop lesbianism.' Written round the side of the banner were the words, 'Turn to Jesus.'

Now, Mr H had preached for over thirty years and had never been subjected to an attack. In fact, the street preacher had been a common sight in this land until it was 'de-religionised' in the mid-1970s.

But as he spoke, the scene suddenly turned ugly. A group of thirty to forty young people who were either homosexuals or their sympathisers surrounded Mr H and sought to silence him by physical force. They assaulted him and threw him to the ground. They threw water over him and tore his banner down.

Picture the scene: a 68-year-old man, standing alone, viciously assaulted by a crowd of young people. A few years before, such a scene would have been inconceivable, no matter what comments an elderly man might make. This would be an extraordinary enough story as it is, but it became even more so.

Convicted

The police were soon on the scene. I should note that the police in this distant land are doing the best they can, but they understand that certain 'hate speech' (that is, if it is anti-Jewish or anti-Christian in tone) is approved and other 'hate speech' is impermissible. Thus, they proceeded to arrest the victim of the assault (Mr H) on the premise that he had 'incited' the attack on his person and that consequently, the assault was justifiable.

In two controversial court cases, it was held that there was a need to show 'tolerance' to the homosexual and lesbian communities and that Mr H's comments were unacceptable. The court recognised the religious significance of his comments and noted that there had been no incitement to violence. The fact that the words were deemed 'insulting', however, sufficed. Mr H died in August 2002, and had he not been convicted by the court, an attempt might have been made to open a murder investigation.

Mr H was convicted of an offence, was fined £300 and had to pay £395 costs, and his placard was destroyed. The reasoning of the court is summarised in paragraph 6 of their decision, which reads

> There was a pressing social need for the restriction and the restriction corresponded to that need: the words on the appellant's sign were directed specifically towards the homosexual community, implying that they were immoral,

and there is a need to show tolerance towards all sections of society; the sign was displayed in the town centre on a Saturday afternoon, provoking hostility from members of the public.

Mr H appealed this decision before his death. The controversial ruling was upheld by the High Court of this strange land. The salient parts of the judgement are recorded in paragraphs 10 and 32. Paragraph 10 reads

> Reading what the sign says and looking at the photograph of it, it is evident that it was not a threatening sign and the case has not been put on the basis that it was abusive. It is, however, put on the basis that this was an insulting sign.

Paragraph 32 of the judgement says

> I have not found this question easy because it is certainly correct that the words on the sign are short and, so far as they go, are not expressed in intemperate language. I have considered very carefully whether this court ought to conclude, in effect, that the words on the sign are incapable of being held, as a matter of fact, to be insulting, but I have come to the clear conclusion that it was open to these magistrates to reach the conclusion that they did, not least because the words on the sign appear to relate homosexuality and lesbianism to immorality.

Thus, the findings of the lower and appeal courts clearly established that the words used by Mr H on his placard were neither threatening nor abusive, neither was any 'intemperate' language used. However, the message on the placard was 'insulting', because it related homosexuality and lesbianism to immorality.

In short, it was the message itself that was 'insulting' and had to be suppressed. The issue in question was whether religious individuals can refer to homosexuality as immoral, and whether they should have to face 'justified' assault if they do.

Mr H was attacked, injured and prosecuted because in this distant land, the words of the Bible are regarded as 'hate speech'. His attackers, mainly young men in their twenties, are free to walk the streets and to attack any elderly citizen who mentions Christian ethics. The national media (with the exception of one or two dissenting voices) approved of this result, as it reflected the morality of this primitive country.

Reality

Now it is time to make the link between this seemingly unlikely story and reality. It will perhaps not surprise you that this distant and primitive land is, of course, the United Kingdom, Mr H is Mr Harry Hammond and the case is DPP v Hammond of 13 January 2004. The town was Bournemouth and the assault on Mr Hammond happened in the middle of one day in October 2001, with fellow citizens walking past.

An isolated incident?

Unfortunately not. I fear that the United Kingdom is rapidly becoming a pagan state whose guiding principles appear to be self-determination, sexual libertarianism and the doctrine of 'relative truth'. Unwisely, Mr Hammond transgressed all these societal values and was duly punished. His offence was to preach a duty to God, sexual restraint and the doctrine of absolute truth.

Compare the fate of Mr Hammond with a pro-homosexual demonstration in Trafalgar Square, London, in July 2002, led by Peter Tatchell and Members of Parliament. In this incident, the supporters of homosexual rights read aloud (through a bull-horn) a poem entitled 'The love that dares not speak its name', a homoerotic poem whose sole claim to notoriety is that it depicts a Roman soldier's homosexual experiences with the dead body of the Lord Jesus Christ.

This poem is, understandably, offensive to adherents of the Christian faith. The laws on blasphemy, one of the few restraints on speech in the United Kingdom, are designed to restrict the expression of disparaging anti-Christian statements. In this case, however, the police declined to enforce the blasphemy laws, citing freedom of speech. In fact, they mounted an operation to 'protect' Mr Tatchell, to ensure that he could exercise his right to 'free speech'.

Thus Mr Hammond used 'insulting' speech to 'save souls' and found himself both attacked and arrested, despite not having broken any specific law, while another speech aimed only at insulting Christians was permitted despite the existence of a specific law to prevent it.

These appear to be policies that British people desire. There is an increasing trend of intolerance towards anyone who articulates the traditional Judaeo-Christian position on issues of morality. True, as our society becomes increasingly secularised, there is an increasing number of social issues on which the views of religious people will be controversial: sexual ethics, incest, abortion, divorce, adultery, embryo research and euthanasia, to take just a few examples. People may be unwilling to be subjected to 'moralising' on such issues, especially if they have strong views or personal grievances themselves. But we cannot allow this to restrict and undermine the freedom of religious speech that is our heritage.

7

The Youth Worker: Gavin Calver

Gavin Calver is married to Anne and lives in Halesowen, West Midlands, where they attend a small free church. A graduate of London Bible College, he ran a Youth for Christ gap-year programme alongside Anne and is now Director of Church Resource at Youth for Christ. A regular public speaker, Gavin works with hundreds of churches to equip their youth work. His first book, *Disappointed with Jesus?*, was published in 2004.

Pressures

What pressures are we up against in the UK today, as we unashamedly continue our efforts to declare the Gospel until Christ comes? Some of the difficulties are obvious, others perhaps less so. Yet some of the more hidden, subtle erosions of the church's position in our society could have devastating results. As we look at some of these challenges in this chapter, our aim is not to alarm but to raise awareness

– and ultimately to kick us into greater action so that our efforts in evangelism are not wasted.

Keep Christianity private

As I drove home from a church meeting the other day I was listening to a discussion on the radio. The audience were phoning in their views too, and as I'm a fan of phone-ins it was just my cup of tea. The subject was fascinating: 'Religion: what a waste of time'. There was a panel of three politically correct atheists who seemed to be perfect representatives of our postmodern, New Labour society, all arguing that religion should just be kept locked up in religious buildings, away from the public. The speakers had no problem with anyone of a religious background, so long as they didn't ever consider taking their religion out of the building. They thought that all religious education should be forbidden in schools, all religious activity outside churches should be banned, and religious talk should be eradicated. They also argued that organised religion was the reason for wars and for the break-ups in our society – actually, all the things that are the opposite of what our faith should stand for.

One listener got through on the phone and said, 'Religious people have ruined this country. They talk about love, hope and freedom but bring nothing but the opposite. They speak about making our lives better but just present us with a list of rules to follow. They say they will make life more fun, yet they make it more boring. These religious people are finished, their time is over; they should just stay in their groups.'

The comments were harsh, but I found them interesting because, as you may not be surprised to learn, I deeply disagree with what the panellists were saying. As I listened for about half an hour or so, it was mesmerising to hear almost all the people phoning in appearing to agree with them. Then one brave guy rang in, an evangelist in schools, but they tore him apart. I was not surprised by the reaction he received, because I believe it is symptomatic of our society. And it wasn't the first time I'd seen Christians who aren't confident in their views just shot down in a media context. Christians often seem afraid to challenge the status quo, even when they are clearly right. This creates a number of difficulties for our evangelism. Fair enough, the UK church's PR does little to challenge the negative views that are so widely held, but we need to find a way of promoting ourselves positively. It's all the more important because in recent years it's become increasingly difficult for the Christian voice to get heard. There is no way that this subject would have been discussed on radio with such ferocity ten years ago, or perhaps even five. And without a religious person on the panel? Never.

Why be PC towards everyone but me?

Political correctness is everywhere today, but it is ironic and frustrating that Christianity is the one faith that the public are not politically correct about. It seems so unfair that people will take the Lord's name in vain as often as they want, yet will be supportive and politically correct about homosexuals, Muslims, mediums, even adulterers. We seem to be the only minority group in Britain that no one defends! If you are homophobic, racist, sexist or against another faith, you are in trouble; but if you are anti-Christian, so what?

We have to ask why. Is it our own fault? Perhaps some of it is. Maybe we focus so much on a God of love that it makes us reluctant to confront the pressures and abuse head-on. We seem to have sussed the God of all comfort, love and joy, but what about the God who judges humanity, the God to be feared, the Jesus who turned over tables – have we lost sight of that aspect of his character? There is so much anti-Christian talk, but we sit back and do nothing about it. We have managed to create a picture of a 'dying breed' in the eyes of the world around us, an image of a faith that is stuck in the past, without a future. The flow of hostile words and actions towards us continues, the radio discussion I heard being a prime example, yet few Christians seem to argue with any conviction.

If you went to a marketing consultancy with the church in Britain as your product, they would say, 'For an organisation with such a large market share, you Christians aren't half quiet!' They would tear apart the way we market ourselves. Somehow we need to change the way we do things. We create pressure for ourselves by the way that we promote ourselves. For too long we have been viewed as people like Ned Flanders from *The Simpsons* – outdated, irrelevant, and singing 'Cumbayah'. We need to throw off that image and show people who we really are. Perhaps it is time to ask, 'How are we perceived and how does that need to change?' We are meant to be like Jesus, and while the Jesus I follow is peace-loving, he is also a radical, world-changing revolutionary.

Out with the ark?

It doesn't help our image when increasing numbers of buildings that used to belong to churches are now being used for other purposes. The public sees that Christian congregations have disbanded and now it is carpet shoppers and people looking for a pint who frequent the newly furnished former worship houses. You cannot but wonder what is happening to Christianity in our nation.

I train regularly at a boxing club, because I believe that evangelists need to be in the places where the non-Christians are. The club is part of a much bigger building that used to be a church but is now run-down and horrible – shabbier than anything I have seen in a long time. It is so sad that a boxing club has kept going but a church has gone. Every week over a hundred young guys go in and out of the boxing club, yet the church is closed. It really is a bitter irony, considering how desperately the body of Christ needs to reach out to young men.

I recently found myself watching one of those house makeover programmes, in which a designer was changing three rooms in sixty minutes. Part of the change was a new-look dining room with pews from a disused church building. The designer argued that they had history and were the perfect look: dark wood with space for a hymnbook. The presenter, however, giggled nervously before declaring that they had gone out with the dark ages and were terrible. She actually seemed embarrassed to be dealing with these remnants of a church, and it was sad to watch. Her sentiments seemed to echo the whole attitude towards churches and Christians in our society today. People see the church as something that belongs in the past, that has no place in our 'new-look' world.

Shifts on Sundays

Boy, how things have changed! Sundays are certainly not what they used to be. It must shock our grandparents, our parents even, that the 'church-going' culture has so swiftly evaporated in our country, as new generations no longer follow the old model on a Sunday but instead use their buildings for what would once have been known as 'worldly activities'. Things have even changed in the short time since our boy David Beckham was a lad. Then, if boys wanted to play for the cubs' football team, they had to attend church. Beckham comments in his book, *My Side*, 'I was playing football with the cubs as well, which you could only do if you went to church on Sunday. So all the family – me, mum and dad and my sisters – made sure we were there every time without fail.'[1]

I can identify with Beckham, because I remember that Sundays were very different when I was a kid. Whether we liked it or not, the supermarket was not open. The shopping centres were not the huge palaces that they are today, and they took no Sunday trade. Granted, football teams did play on Sundays and that did cause tension in the family home. But football aside, there wasn't much that happened on a Sunday. If you were religious you went to church, and if you weren't you had family time.

Now a new 'church' has emerged. Merry Hill shopping centre in Dudley, West Midlands, interestingly has two spires coming out of the top of it! Sunday shopping is a huge affair – people go regularly to these cathedrals of consumerism and worship at the altar of the megastore. Yet they leave with no lasting fulfilment.

It's not just shopping that fills our Sundays; there are several other choices, as you can see if you look at a typical schedule for kids' activities these days. The dance group, swimming club or even martial arts class that used to be on a Tuesday is now often at 11 o'clock on a Sunday morning. A children's party which in the past would have taken place on a Saturday afternoon can now easily interrupt old-fashioned family time on a Sunday.

Sunday seems to be no longer sacred or special. The roads that used to be dead are now crammed full of people trying to get to the shops, the cinema or some other place of entertainment. I am not one to say that we should simply be Sunday Christians, but when Sundays were special there was greater Christian freedom and a greater awareness of the church. Today Christianity is no longer part of the landscape in people's minds: it is swiftly being forgotten and replaced by materialism and consumerism. Once upon a time our faith was accepted, and indeed the norm of society, but now it is rapidly being divorced from it. I have been amazed by some of the young people I have met in recent years who do not even know the story of Noah's Ark! Christian Sunday School stories that used to be known by all are now relegated to the archives with old myths and legends.

There used to be some kudos in going to church; it was seen as a good thing to do. The church always provided for social needs. But now it seems that it is an embarrassment, and people no longer associate the church with positive activity, or even perhaps with morality. Things have changed very quickly in a short space of time. People are alienated from the church. There is no word more guaranteed to put people off these days than 'evangelism' or 'evangelist'. People ask me what I do and I tell them that I work for Youth for Christ. There is no hiding that it is an evangelistic organisation. What could be more unpopular, more politically incorrect or socially unacceptable than outright evangelism in Jesus' name?

Schools

When my dad was a young evangelist some thirty years ago, things were very different. Kids were familiar with Bible stories and people were not afraid to endorse Christian teaching. As a young evangelist he had access to schools and anywhere else for evangelism. He was one of the first youth evangelists in this nation and now, ironically, thirty years on, things have gone full circle and they are trying to kick us out. We face a very real pressure in schools these days, and have to be careful not to get ourselves into difficult situations. We have to be sure to say that what we are talking about is what we believe, not that it is objectively true. Sadly, there has to be tact in the way we present the Gospel so that it is not too 'in your face'.

And then there's the confusion of faiths in schools. I often used to see a young relative of mine who was just six years old. He would get very excited when I went round because we were very close to each other. There was one time when I went to see him and he came running up to me shouting 'Hello' at the top of his voice. He was so excited, and he said, 'Guess what? I made a Christingle at school for Hanukkah!' For me, that statement just about sums up the confusion regarding faith at school. The Christingle is a Christian symbol and has nothing to do with the Jewish festival of Hanukkah – it was a complete mixture of religion. Schools have become so pluralistic in the way they present religion that the young child cannot see the wood for the trees.

Many schools teach that all religions are equal and relative, with the result that a six-year-old is deeply and noticeably confused. He or she is presented with aspects of all religions at a very early age and encouraged to think that they are all equally valid. Some schools also believe that the best religious studies teachers are those of no religion. Where will that take us? The fundamental challenge for us as Christians is that our Jesus doesn't compromise in that way; he constantly says that the only way to God is 'through Me'. If he says that he is the way, the truth and the life, he cannot be put on a par with all other faiths. The changing nature of school teaching is directly contradicting the words of our Lord.

Confusing faiths

The confusion we find in the minds of children at school can also unfortunately be found in other generations. When I was chatting with my neighbour the other day she explained to me that every one of her children has been christened and that the church in our town is really special to her. Then she went on to tell me how the little Buddha in her garden brings peace to it. This is a prime example of the sheer confusion that people are living in. One minute, celebrities are thanking God for their awards, and the next minute they are talking about idols and shrines that re-energise them for their work. We have replaced the idea of belonging to a specific religion with a postmodern eclectic mix of faiths chosen by the individual. It is all about pleasing my soul, doing what feels good, and answering my immediate needs. The one thing they don't seem to look at is

Christianity – the one thing that can provide them with ultimate truth.

Here is the challenge that confronts us: how do we show that our faith is different in a world that tries to convince us that they are all the same? If you want to do Christian outreach in areas such as Bradford, Leeds or London, you are under a great deal of pressure because so many faiths are represented. In London's Leicester Square representatives of every faith jump on you, all wanting to provide the answer, and it is hard for people to know which way to turn. In this environment, how do we show that Jesus Christ is the answer? Well, we cannot compromise. We cannot just be nice to people and afraid to be different. We still need to use proclamation of the truth in our evangelism, and we cannot allow the confusion about faiths in our society to dilute our message.

Don't quit

It is not all negative, however. There are some great positives at work in the face of these modern pressures. Just look at the work that Alpha is doing across the UK and the wider world. Alpha has gained respect from many people in Britain, even from non-believers, because it has done something very significant in many people's lives.

I was greatly encouraged when chatting to a schools worker recently. She said that in one of the local schools where her schools project operates the head of religious education is a Hindu. After building a relationship with her for two years, the Christians are now allowed to come in and do whatever they want. The chains have been taken off.

There are no reins, there are no rules, and a relationship has been built. The Hindu may have different beliefs but she has built trust with the schools worker. Hallelujah – a bridge – a way in! In Youth for Christ we have found that while there is restrictive legislation, if you can build relationships with schools there is a way.

There is a shortage of teachers, so if a group like YFC offers to take some lessons, do learning support groups or take PE lessons it can be a great blessing for a school. It is a case of making the most of the opportunities that we are given. The irony of the situation, it seems to me, is that there is more and more legislation and negativity, yet our schools work seems to be going from strength to strength. In some areas schools are more open than ever before, with some local YFC schools workers being given carte blanche to work with them. We just need creative new initiatives to reach people. One of our newer resources, *The Art of Connecting*, trains young people in how to engage in evangelism. We may be hitting barriers in getting adults into schools, but no one can stop a kid who loves Jesus sharing his faith. After all, this is what we're supposed to do!

Some of the pressures in evangelism today have helped to make us ask ourselves what evangelism is. It is not about five or six preachers in a town; it is actually about everyone who believes in Jesus getting off their backsides and sharing him. The pressure of not having an open-air location to witness in, or a football stadium for an event, or even the finance for such an operation, has made us say, 'What are we going to do, then?' It has led to things such as developing market place ministry, empowering young people to minister in schools, and finally to a body of believers beginning to share the truth of Christ in the workplace. In some contexts, especially in schools, we require a subtle approach to Christianity, but in other situations such as in clubs and on streets we can adopt a more overt stance. We need to be sensitive without compromising our beliefs.

I do believe that if the whole body of the church does not start sharing the Gospel in the next ten years, then yes, the picture may be bleak, and the pressures we are up against will harm us deeply. But if we do find new ways, just imagine what could happen. Society will be hit from all sides because no one can stop the Spirit moving through God's people.

---

[1] Beckham, David, *My Side* (London: Harper Collins Willow, 2003), 23.

8

The Persecuted Church: Eddie Lyle

Eddie Lyle is Chief Executive of the Christian agency Release International, which serves persecuted Christians in thirty countries around the world by supporting pastors and their families, supplying Christian literature and Bibles and working for justice. Previously he was director of Youth for Christ in Scotland and served on the YFC National Leadership Team for seven years, with responsibility for discipleship training and mobilisation programmes in the UK and overseas. Born in Northern Ireland, Eddie now lives in Scotland with his wife Christine and son Adam.

Exodus

My motorcycle joined the hundreds of others making their way out of the Vietnamese Central Highlands township at the end of the day. As darkness arrived, this was the perfect time for me to be 'spirited' out of the area. A gentle rain started to fall.

I must have been surrounded by thousands of people on their way home through the rush hour traffic, sometimes six to one motorcycle. Young women in chiffon scarves, wearing sequin-embroidered evening gloves to guard their skin against the cold night air, raced past us, adding a surreal sense to this most unusual of travelling experiences.

My route had been checked and rechecked during the day. I was still nervous. I was unaccustomed to the pillion position on a Yamaha 125, and even more inexperienced in bobbing and weaving through the sea of other vehicles. I clung for life to the church pastor who had agreed to take me to meet his congregation. We struggled through traffic for almost an hour, before hitting the darkness of the main road north. I settled back and prayed for inspiration. As I mounted the motorcycle, the pastor had asked if I would bring God's word to his people.

A few miles out of town we left the main road and followed dirt tracks for what seemed an eternity. Then, just as the rain began to ease, we entered a jungle clearing in pitch darkness. As we picked our way through the night, the silhouette of a large building on stilts emerged.

Underground

I climbed a tree trunk notched with steps and suddenly there I was: my first encounter with the underground church. In front of me were two hundred people. It was also their first encounter with a Western Christian, and spontaneous applause erupted as we entered the hall.

For two hours we shared God's word with one another, sang hymns and prayed for the church. In recent weeks, security forces had closed churches, securing the doors with chains and padlocks. Closure notices had been pasted to front walls.

Yet there was no sense of panic, more a quiet sense of resignation to what had been expected for some time. The fact that we were meeting outside the town in a remote jungle location was proof positive that direst persecution of the church in this area was a very real issue. Many had walked for up to four hours to be at this service.

Pastor S told me of his weekly interrogation by the police. I asked him how he felt when the police questioned him. 'No fear,' he said. 'Look what's happening here. God is at work, and I have no need to be frightened. They have tried to close us down, and look what has happened!'

Had he a message for the church in the West? 'Ask them to remember us. We need your prayers so that we can withstand the pressure of persecution. Today we have over 140,000 children in our Sunday schools in this region. Could you help us to get some flannelgraphs to teach the children?' (A flannelgraph is a felt storyboard, with figures and a colourful background, used to tell Bible stories.)

Pastor S was to be the first of a number of remarkable people I would meet over the next few days, working with the Vietnamese church. Most of my meetings were at night, when Christians could use the cover of darkness to travel discreetly.

A small group of Hmong people, who have long suffered persecution and the onslaught of ethnic cleansing in several South-East Asian countries, had travelled at great personal risk to meet me. Their native costume of black with exquisite embroidery displayed all that remains of their cultural heritage. What do you say to people who have literally lost everything because of their determination to follow Jesus?

Expelled by the Vietnamese communist authorities from their native territory, they are now homeless and eke out a basic existence, relying on other Christians to buy food for them, as they cannot speak Vietnamese.

Forced labour

Supporting these people was Pastor A, who had recently been freed after seven-and-a-half years in prison. He told of how he had experienced the Lord's sustaining grace while in a labour camp, where he was forced to carry two thousand bricks a day, surviving on just four bowls of rice and one cup of water.

Today Pastor A is a significant leader in the underground church, overseeing the training of young leaders and the printing and distribution of Bibles. His ordeal has somehow created a very gracious and humble man, who was obviously highly regarded by his contemporaries and who is passionate about the Gospel.

Sister C was recently released from prison after four-and-a-half years. Her crime had been to lead two entire villages to Christ, and to make inroads into a region with the Gospel. Again, she recounted harrowing stories of her imprisonment. It was painful to hear; and I can't imagine what it must have been like to experience. But the result is a growing and radiant Christian quite prepared, in her own words, to go through it all again for the sake of following Christ and spreading his word.

These are just some of the human stories behind a deteriorating situation that deserves an outcry by those who cherish the most basic ingredient of human rights: the right to worship and express one's religious faith without fear of intimidation or harassment.

Growing persecution

In spite of intense monitoring and advocacy by international human rights organisations and religious liberties groups alike, the Vietnamese authorities have continued their 'strike hard' tactics against the church.

On 18 June 2004 the Standing Committee of the National Assembly issued an official Ordinance on Religion, No. 21/2004/PL-UBTVQH 11, which came into effect on 15 November 2004. This ordinance creates many problems and disadvantages for the church, especially regarding gatherings for worship. The legislation provides a legal basis for local authorities to hinder and persecute the church, particularly house churches, which have not been recognised since 1975.

This is a desperately serious situation because in the past, even without this measure, local authorities have treated the house churches very badly. Now the authorities have new powers to persecute 800,000 tribal believers in the Central Highlands and Northern mountains, and about 300,000 house church believers in the lowlands and the cities.

My new Vietnamese Christian friends and my first experience of the 'underground church' taught me a valuable lesson about not taking our freedoms for granted. It is all too easy for us in the West to undervalue the freedom we enjoy to meet and worship without restriction. Who knows, but in years to come some of these basic freedoms may even be challenged in our own nation.

Pakistan: Nageena's story

Her mother was the only one to hear her story. The seven-year-old whispered it once, and since then has hardly talked at all.

She was returning from a friend's house at 11:30 a.m., when someone called out. As she turned, four men from her village ran towards her. Nageena ran too, tripping on her scarf, stumbling on the unmade road. She is not sure why she ran – because they were running, because they had never spoken to her, because the only man she had ever talked to was her father. But the four men were faster, cornering her, catching her.

She could remember being pushed through a wooden door into a dark room. She had screamed, but could not describe what happened next.

Villagers heard her crying and a crowd gathered outside the cowshed. Ghulam Masih saw the commotion, ran over and pulled open the door. Inside he saw his neighbour's four sons standing over his daughter, her clothes tangled with straw, her legs covered with blood. As he scooped Nageena into his arms, the four men backed away and ran across a field.

Nageena's father and mother carried their daughter to the police station, filed a criminal complaint and were put on a bus to Shekhupura Hospital, in Pakistan's Punjab province. It was 10:30 p.m. by the time they arrived. The duty doctor's medical report concluded that Nageena's internal injuries were so severe that she would never be able to have children.

Over the next two weeks, as Nageena hid under her hospital blanket, the Sharqpur police arrested the four men, after dozens of villagers came forward with their names.

It would be another six weeks before Nageena spoke again to her mother, and when she did it was to ask why the four rapists were back in the village.

The police had freed them and closed the case. The inspector said he could find no evidence and told Nageena's family to forget the matter. But Ghulam continued to demand justice and refused gifts of a new home, money, sweets and clothes from the men who had raped his daughter.

Nineteen months later, the family thought their determination had paid off. They received a letter from a new government department, the Human Rights Ministry of Pakistan, which said it had reviewed the criminal file and had decided to award Nageena £200 compensation.

Accused

Two weeks later, Ghulam Masih was back at Sharqpur police station. This time he was lying half-naked with his face in the dirt, iron chains around his wrists and ankles. The police were beating Ghulam in order to extract a confession. He was accused of killing an old woman, and his accusers were his daughter's rapists.

Why had the word of four men who were accused of the rape of a child been acted upon without investigation, while the report of Nageena's assault gathered dust in the inspector's office?

'The prisoner is a Christian,' the inspector said, 'and the men who are accused of raping his daughter are good Muslims. I have no reason to disbelieve them, as they are good Muslims. My first duty is to Islam. The courts will take a similar view and Ghulam Masih will be hanged. You'll see.'

After Ghulam had been detained for fourteen days, a Lahore High Court bailiff rushed to the prison and forced an order into the police inspector's hands. Ghulam was freed but the charge against him still remains. For security reasons he now has to live in hiding and Nageena has found safety in a Christian sanctuary.

The story of Nageena and Ghulam seems difficult to believe: a little girl, mute from assault; a father facing a death sentence for pursuing justice.

Nageena was raped because she was a Christian. In the eyes of her attackers her religion made her worthless, vulnerable and unlikely to be believed. Her father is facing a death sentence because he dared to challenge a judicial system in which the word of a Muslim is officially worth more than that of a Christian.

When I met Nageena, she was 12 years old and part of a worship group at a seminar to help women see their value in God. The five years that have passed since this incident have brought a measure of healing, although there is still a long way to go. As I watched her caught up in worship, I marvelled at God's goodness in restoring her to the extent that she can now be involved in leading others into the healing presence of God.

Nageena is safe, but I would meet many more over the next few days who were not so fortunate.

Emmanuel

When Emmanuel Bhatti walked into my room, I stood to welcome him with an embrace, but to my embarrassment I saw that his arms were paralysed. Overcoming the awkward moment, I greeted him in Jesus' name. Accompanying him was his twelve-year-old son.

On 3 February 1999, Emmanuel, who had been active in social work in his area, was accused of kidnapping. While detained in the police station, he was hung from the ceiling of a torture cell for seven days and beaten repeatedly. When he was cut down, a concrete roller was pushed over his legs, arms and backbone. So severe were his injuries, he now has no use of his arms. His young son now functions as his arms, to feed him and help him in the bathroom.

Until recently, Emmanuel's two sons worked in a local soap factory for twelve hours a day as the principal breadwinners for the Bhatti family. Even now, the family members have to endure harassment and threats.

Although legal action was taken against the police officials involved, the Lahore High Court has yet to give a verdict on the petition which was submitted, nor are they likely to, judging by present practice.

The injustices suffered by the Christian community in Pakistan are some of the cruellest that I have witnessed. In my time in the Punjab, I met with over sixty people who were victims of Pakistan's discriminatory legal system, including the archaic Blasphemy Law (295c), which is often used punitively against innocent Christians and others.

Yet in the midst of this pervasively destructive environment, I met with many who were passionate about living openly for Christ.

Love

I think of Pastor Hezekiel Shoorosh, leading a church of over two thousand people in a fundamentalist enclave of Lahore. His testimony is remarkable. In 1987 God gave him a vision to start a church, which initially met in his home.

Fundamentalists heard of the fledgling congregation and a mob turned up at his door to bring an end to the church and to kill him. He bowed to the leader of the gang, a doctor, and invited the entire group into his home for refreshments.

The group could not understand his behaviour and frantically retreated to discuss tactics. The leader re-emerged to say that they declined his hospitality and that they were leaving him in peace. To this day, no one has threatened the pastor in this way.

Hezekiel said, 'They tried to kill me, but I killed them with the love of God.'

I visited the church to speak at their Friday evening meeting, which was an integral part of the church's weekly three days of prayer and fasting. To hear their prayers for spiritual awakening in Lahore and to join in with their worship was one of the greatest privileges of my life.

I think also of a grandmother who told me how assailants broke into her home in order to take her life. She knelt before the one with the cudgel and began to pray that God would accept her soul as she stepped into eternity. As the man wielded the club and brought it down upon her head, he was stopped by an invisible hand, and fled the house, screaming hysterically.

When I asked her what was the most beautiful thing about the Lord Jesus Christ, she started to weep copiously and said, 'My salvation. He stepped out of the glory of heaven, and from the presence of the Father, to save my soul.' I shared in her tears. Her face glowed with such immense peace and grace.

Jesus said to his twelve disciples in Matthew 10:28, 'Do not be afraid of those who kill the body but cannot kill the soul.'

I have found there is a rare beauty in the lives of persecuted Christians, from which we can all draw encouragement and inspiration.

Time and again, I have met those for whom these words of Christ were no vain hyperbole. They are words of life, to be both believed and lived.

Watchful

My experiences over these several challenging days in Pakistan were intensified by the fact that my visit coincided with the anniversary of the birth of the prophet Muhammad. It seemed as though every mullah in Lahore was in his minaret, either preaching or praying.

Every newspaper stand had the photographs of Iraqi prisoners being tortured by US forces. We cancelled our plans to film prayers at a local mosque because tensions were running high.

Visiting the Lahore High Court exposed me to the culture and background of the Pakistani legal system. It was established and modelled by the British, and many of the vestiges of a now long-forgotten past are still easily identifiable. Yet how could something established on the tenets of the Ten Commandments now be one of the most corrupt legal systems in the world, with Christians being among those most vilified?

Late one evening my team and I had tea with a prominent bishop from the Church of Pakistan. I asked him where he felt the church was in terms of its relationship with the wider community. With considerable honesty, he replied, 'We are floating between desire and fear.' The desire to stand up against growing persecution and to witness for Christ, set against the quite warranted fear of attack by armed militants.

This man, who had endured significant intimidation and threat, and who had helped many who had been forced to flee their homes and livelihoods, was speaking out of the reality of his situation. To be a Christian today in Pakistan is a dangerous calling; especially as militant organisations increasingly see local indigenous churches as 'soft targets' in their global jihad.

While everything is not perfect in the UK, equality before the law and a police force and judiciary free of blatant corruption and discrimination are things we may easily take for granted. Yet in Pakistan these institutions, instead of protecting the Christian and other minorities, are increasingly becoming tools of persecution and abuse.

In our own situations we should be prayerfully watchful concerning how the legal system is used, ensuring that basic freedoms and rights are maintained for all members of the community, regardless of creed, race or gender.

Three phases of persecution

As we observe the persecution of Christians around the world, whether at the hands of repressive authorities or militant groups, we can identify three distinct phases of activity: disinformation, discrimination and outright violence.

Disinformation is when false propaganda is spread about Christian communities, often through irresponsible media. This may serve to stir up popular feelings against Christians, especially if they are in a minority, and may reinforce negative cultural stereotypes. For example, we have seen this recently in Sri Lanka, where extremist Buddhists have waged a concerted campaign of disinformation to portray Christianity as an enemy of Buddhist culture, religion and language. Seventy-three Christian organisations have been accused of engaging in 'unethical conversions' and anti-Buddhist activity.

Discrimination is when Christians are treated as 'second-class citizens', as we have seen in Pakistan. Christians who are being discriminated against have a poorer legal, social, economic and political standing than those who profess the majority religion. In these circumstances Christians are often viewed with suspicion as traitors to their nation.

The third stage of outright violence is what happens when intense persecution takes place with impunity, with Christians denied the normal protection of the law. We have seen this recently, for example, in Plateau State, Nigeria, where Christian communities are periodically violently assaulted and displaced, yet no perpetrators have been brought to justice. States and regional authorities themselves may also act in this way against Christians, as we can see today, for example, in China, North Korea and Vietnam.

As we continue to support and pray for persecuted Christians around the world, let us also be vigilant in our own nation and community. History has shown that the progression from disinformation to violence can be surprisingly rapid.

The Politician: Ram Gidoomal

An entrepreneur and former UK Group Chief Executive of the Inlaks Group, Ram Gidoomal was a member of the independently appointed Cabinet Office Better Regulation Task Force and chaired the Anti-Discrimination Legislation and Local Shops sub-groups. He is Chairman of Employability Forum and a council member of the Institute for Employment Studies, and is the author of several books, including *The UK Maharajahs* and *The British and how to deal with them: Doing business with Britain's Ethnic Communities*. Ram stood as the Christian People's Alliance candidate for London Mayor in 2000 and 2004, polling nearly one hundred thousand votes on both occasions.

Legislation

How effective is legislation as a tool to bring about social change?

We live in a time of increasing legislation. The courts are seen as the most effective way both to enhance and to protect our individual freedoms.

The acknowledgement of the European Court of Human Rights as having sovereignty over our laws, together with the influence of the American emphasis on litigation in every area of life, has played no small part in this process.

While the rule of law is one of the foundational pillars of a free society, the actual passing of laws is not always the most appropriate way to address sensitive issues. Laws passed with good intentions can have unintended consequences that actually threaten freedom.

For example:

- We are seeing the passage of employment legislation that will oblige Christian bodies to employ non-Christians. This European law will bring Christian organisations into costly litigation. On one level, of course, this is a threat to the freedom that religious organisations have traditionally enjoyed. But it also brings with it a more insidious possibility: that in the process of defending that freedom some Christian organisations might be bankrupted. Just as Premier Radio was challenged to review whether its language was prejudiced against Satanists, it is not unreasonable to assume that there are humanists waiting to take a class action against the weakest Christian body they can find, with the aim of bringing us all swiftly to heel.

- Secondly, we are seeing an attack on church schools, supported by parties historically compelled by humanitarianism and tolerance. In a hard-hitting article for the *Catholic Herald* in February 2002, Lord Alton warned that the threat from what he called the 'latter-day Robespierres' was a very real one, to be ignored at our peril.

- Thirdly, we are seeing, across a broad range of key moral issues, a government consensus backed by the scientific establishment, shoring up a wide range of anti-biblical positions.

A vivid example has been the Government's backing for new legislation to combat religious hatred and discrimination on the basis of religion. While everybody is (or should be) opposed to discrimination on the basis of religion, race or any other personal aspect of our lives, it is not so clear that legislation is the best way to prevent it.

The nearest parallel is the legislation against discrimination on the basis of race, which has been strengthened by amendments in 2000 to include a public sector duty to promote equality.

Limitations of law

The record of this legislation is mixed. On the one hand it has sent a clear signal that our society treats all its citizens alike and that discrimination on personal grounds is not tolerated. This was much needed and there have been positive changes in our society as a result. We are seeing increasing efforts by public sector bodies to respond to the needs of minority ethnic communities and making efforts to ensure that their leadership at all levels reflects the communities they serve.

On the other hand it can be notoriously difficult to interpret and implement, especially in cases where a motive of racial prejudice or discrimination is alleged. The law is based on the perception of the person who feels discriminated against, and this is by definition subjective. Many cases that have gone to employment tribunals, for example, have ended in even greater bitterness and a climate in which people are constantly looking for excuses to attack another person or to claim victimisation.

This is not to say that we do not need legislation against racial discrimination, but it is to point out the limited ability of law, by itself, to change attitudes, and the unexpected consequences which some laws can have.

What about religious discrimination? The same cautions apply. The new legislation sets out to ban direct and indirect discrimination that treats a person less favourably on the grounds of religion or belief. That seems fair enough. It also aims to restrict victimisation 'where someone is treated less favourably than others because, for example, they have complained of discrimination or have assisted someone else in a complaint'. That brings us into areas similar to those covered by the laws on racial discrimination, with probably the same mixed results.

So far, we are simply saying that laws are not a simple solution to changing attitudes and preventing bad practices, such as discrimination.

Divided reactions

The Government included legislation against religious hatred as part of a package of measures against terrorism in the wake of the 9/11 attacks (11 September 2001). This clause was one of several removed by the House of Lords at that time, but on 7 July 2004, David Blunkett, then Home Secretary, announced that the Government was planning to introduce a new law banning incitement to religious hatred. Reasons included the growing racism on the grounds of religion and the expression of extremist beliefs post-9/11. The Home Office said that the proposed measures would cover a 'gap' in Britain's laws, whereby people who make inflammatory remarks against Jews and Sikhs (groups with both religious and ethnic identities) can be prosecuted, but anyone making comments that would inflame hatred against Christians, Muslims, Hindus and other religions (which do not constitute ethnic groups) is exempt from prosecution.

The Home Secretary argued that his proposals would protect ordinary people who want to get on with following their faith and would 'sideline' extremists who claim to speak for them. While the media tends to focus on Islamic radicals, the Government stressed that the law would 'apply equally to far-right Christian evangelicals' and other faiths if words were used that could lead to acts of violence.

Responses to this proposal (as distinct from the laws against discrimination) were sharply divided.

Some, like Trevor Philips, Chair of the Commission for Racial Equality, expressed support for the proposals, agreeing that there were many who did not have the full protection of anti-discrimination laws.

Some Muslim organisations which had campaigned for a change in the law welcomed the proposals. Others expressed fears over how the laws might be used against minority groups. Rather than enjoying additional protection from the law, religious minorities could find themselves the targets of prosecution.

Dr Ghayasuddin Siddiqui, leader of the Muslim Parliament, said, 'We are not looking forward to legislation which will change nothing, except that the first victim will be a Muslim.'

The chief executive of the National Secular Society, Keith Porteous Wood, said that the new laws would be 'yet another blow to freedom of expression'.

Labour peer Lord Desai believed there was no need for the new measures: 'We will get into a real muddle if we take religion as a ground for prosecution, rather than ethnic stereotyping. When people insult Muslims they are not attacking the religion, they are attacking Muslims as a racial group. The protection required is already covered in law.'

Looking at this particular law helps to sharpen our original question: 'How effective is legislation as a tool to bring about social change? Can passing a law really win hearts and minds and overcome the prejudice and racism that fuel hatred and incite violence in society?' As a former member of the Cabinet Office Better Regulation Task Force, I believe that more legislation is not the answer. Surely what is needed is a delicate balance, in which legal intervention seems less likely to be helpful. The Government is generally very positive towards faith communities and recognises their value. It rightly wants to prevent religious discrimination and religious hatred. But is legislation the best way to tackle these problems?

The case for self-regulation

I believe a more effective way is self-regulation. What does this involve?

We need to agree, as Christians, that we really are committed to removing religious hatred and all other kinds of offensive attitude or behaviour from our society. If we are, we should also agree to take steps to avoid anything in our words or actions that causes unnecessary offence. And we should work together with others to develop, as far as possible, an agreed framework within which we all operate.

Christians have not always been good at this. We have been so convinced of the truth of what we believe, and so opposed to error, that we have often spoken and acted in ways that have condemned others or been insensitive to their beliefs and practices.

Before we spell out what this means in practice, we need to consider some questions. Firstly, is this another form of political correctness, which can result in inhibiting truthful speech and actually make relationships worse? No, it is 'speaking the truth in love', a principle which the apostle Paul described as the mark of Christian maturity (Eph. 4:13–15).

Secondly, isn't religion a private matter? As Christians, do we have any right to impose our views on others, especially in our pluralist multifaith society?

Christian faith is not just a private belief, though many are arguing for the privatisation of religion. The late Bishop Lesslie Newbigin often spoke of the Gospel of Christ as 'public truth in the public square': his definition of 'public truth' was 'that which all people should acknowledge as true – because it is true'. But today we are moving in a very different direction, to a place where one's religious faith, even if one is in government, is a purely private matter and has no bearing on the public decisions one makes. The Christian church is at the beginning of a culture war, roughly in the same place as the USA was at the end of the 1990s.

But if our faith is 'public truth', how do we practise it in our plural society?

We cannot force people to respect Christianity, far less to adopt it, simply because they live in a supposedly 'Christian country'. We do, as Christians, have a responsibility to develop social interaction, working relationships and a platform for discussion of religious and spiritual issues with neighbours who do not share our faith.

Living in a plural society, with the conviction that our faith is true, we need all the more to commit ourselves to expressing our faith, sharing our values and turning them into social policies, in ways that are sensitive, courteous and respectful of others who do not share all our beliefs. Some will be actively opposed, while others will agree with us in some areas and not others.

We are in a very similar situation to that in which the apostle Paul saw his ministry flourish under God, for example in the city of Ephesus, which was dedicated to a pagan goddess whose image was to be seen everywhere and whose followers were numerous. There were other gods and goddesses in Ephesus, and the city was as unlikely a setting for a great expansion of the kingdom as you could imagine. But in Acts 19 we read how Paul's ministry extended over the whole province. How? Well, he didn't do it by attacking other faiths and trying to tear down those statues.

Paul simply set out his stall. He saw Ephesus as a market place and he set about demonstrating the supreme quality of what he had on his own stall. He did not campaign for the Gospel; he merely taught it in a strongly pagan city, and the whole province heard it (and a thriving idol industry was ruined!).

A place to stand

Christians possess a belief system – enshrined in Scripture – that is morally and intellectually sound. Not only can we introduce people to the Saviour, we can also give honest answers to honest questions. In a world that is full of doubt and is searching for answers, Christianity can talk on the basis of real, defensible authority. In public life, it can be a priceless advantage to know that in the frequent moral mazes of local government, for example, there is such a concept as 'meaning', and that it is not nonsense to talk about there being such a thing as 'truth'.

And so we have a place to stand in a confusing and shifting world. We can remain firm in a society in which many faiths press many claims. We do not have to despise or be discourteous to other faiths, but neither do we have to remain helpless in the face of their messages. The world is crying out for moral certitude and absolute principles.

The absolute revelation of Scripture frees us from relative morality and situational ethics. We can make absolute judgements and call things objectively right or wrong, because we live by an objective moral law. That doesn't mean that we know all the answers, but we do know that it is not nonsense to look for answers, and that there is a source of truth who can be known. This faith-assumption easily translates into concrete social policies.

What do people of other faiths think of this? One answer is certainly indicated by my own experiences in the London

Mayoral campaign. While the Christian establishment hesitated to lend its support, Hindus, Muslims and Sikhs backed my campaign with more than words.

They gave money, campaigned for us and sent public endorsements. They were absolutely delighted to see a political party openly speaking up for pro-life issues, family life and so on. There was much integrity in this support, for none of those from other faiths was suggesting that faith was unimportant or that the distinctives of different religions were immaterial. But they were attracted by the policies which were based on our Christian values.

The Fantasy Mayor website set up by the *New Statesman* made the point brilliantly. On entering the website, 3.5 per cent of the visitors indicated their intention to vote for the Christian People's Alliance (CPA) and 56 per cent indicated their preference for Ken Livingstone. Fifteen policy questions to do with a wide range of issues were then posed, from health, transport and education to disability, unemployment and policing.

The answers to these questions showed a surprising result. The CPA came out top, matching 24 per cent of the answers of the visitors. Ken Livingstone's policies scored a mere 6 per cent. *The Times* said that if this election were to be fought on policies alone, the Christian People's Alliance would win by a landslide!

Foundations of law

So, you might ask, are you saying that all our laws must be based on Christian beliefs? Here is my response:

- British law has always been Christian-based. The laws of England, Wales, Scotland and Northern Ireland all derive from the Bible, and have done so for centuries. Here, for example, is the philosopher Jeremy Bentham, commenting on William Blackstone's *Commentaries on the Laws of England* (1775): 'The Laws of Nature and Revelation: hapless the man that does not understand them now. These are our foundations. "Upon these two foundations, depend all human Laws."' To use a metaphor from Soren Kierkegaard, 'You cannot sew without first tying a knot in the thread.' Christianity, so far as British law is concerned, is the knot in the legal thread.

- It is this Judaeo-Christian foundation of law that protects in a way that mere ethics cannot. For example, the ultimate task of Parliament is to frame a body of law that will protect the freedoms of the individual, but on the basis of absolute principles, not just the wishes of the majority. Even when the party in power has an unassailable majority and can push through any legislation it wants to, it is not free to do so without taking these principles into account.

- What we are seeing today is a move to a rights-based, individualised political and legal framework that owes more to the French Revolution than to the tradition of common law that has guided our country's judiciary for centuries. It is based on the views of the majority (which of course change from year to year), rather than on principles to which even the majority are subject.

- A rights-based system can easily drive Christianity back into the cupboard, by insisting that Christianity is just one minority faith among many others.

- But at every point the Gospel seeks to limit the absolute power of the state and provide effective checks, by recognising that the responsibility for ordering and regulating our lives in society does not belong to government alone. There are different spheres and a whole range of non-government structures – family, business, arts, religious bodies, voluntary associations – which have different responsibilities. We often refer to this range of structures and institutions as 'civil society'. When they are strong, society is healthy, because there are adequate checks and balances and we are not dependent only on the state or 'the Government' to do everything for us.

So how do we put self-regulation into practice? Here are three principles to guide us.

1. Code of practice

Consult with other Christians to agree on the need and draw up a draft code of practice. This would include guidelines for how we relate to people of other beliefs (of any kind: religious, political or cultural).

Here is one example, published by Faith to Faith, a Christian consultancy for relating to people of other faiths. It is based on the Ten Commandments:

TEN COMMITMENTS FOR FAITH TO FAITH

Relying on the grace of God, and acknowledging that we will often fall short, we recognise the One True God as He who has given us salvation through Christ, and we worship and serve only Him.

We recognise and repent of all false worship by ourselves and other Christians – including giving too much honour to ethnicity and culture as well as accepting the norms of the belief systems that surround us where they oppose the Gospel.

We take care not to put ourselves into the place of God by offering judgements on His behalf.

We seek to order our own households in a way that centres on God and respects all people. The minorities in our communities should be treated in the same way as the majority.

We are people as part of their community and not only as individuals, and give due honour to family ties and responsibilities.

We do not respond to people out of anger or hatred; we never insult people, and we always seek reconciliation if we find that we have offended others.

We continually examine our own lives, and seek to live in purity and holiness.

We seek economic and social justice, and do not make our own welfare our priority.

We speak only the truth. In speaking of other faiths, we take seriously the way their adherents describe them, and avoid unfair comparisons.

We do not act out of envy, but genuinely rejoice when others have good things.[1]

2. Agreement

Consult with people of other beliefs, share the draft code of practice with them, and seek to come to common agreement as far as possible – even seeking to draw up effective whistle-blowing policies!

3. Public opinion

Work to change public opinion. We have already seen how important this is. As C.S. Lewis memorably said, we shall never have a Christian society until the majority of people want one. And that does not mean a society in which only one voice is heard. As Howard Peskett, Vice-Principal of Trinity College, Bristol, said in a letter to the Home Secretary in November 2001

> It is essential in a free and civilised society that people are allowed to disagree, and to debate those disagreements, especially about their deepest beliefs (which include religious beliefs). At the same time they must be taught and led to conduct those disagreements with courtesy and respect. We can encourage this freedom under a general canopy of 'chartered pluralism', by teaching rights, responsibilities and respect.[2]

Our conversations with those of other faiths can take place in the context of mutual citizenship, of shared civic concerns, of joint seeking for social justice and defending the powerless. We can be what Francis Schaeffer called 'co-belligerents', for we share many points of commitment with others who do not share our commitment to the truth of Christianity but who wholeheartedly share many lesser agendas with us.

---

1 Faith to Faith newsletter, July 2001. Reproduced with permission.

2 Published in Faith to Faith newsletter, December 2001.

The Sociologist: Nick Spencer

Nick Spencer read Modern History and English at Oxford and works as a researcher and writer for the London Institute for Contemporary Christianity and for the Jubilee Centre. His major interest lies in exploring how social, cultural and intellectual trends relate to the Christian faith today. He writes widely for the Christian press and is the author of a number of books, most recently on asylum and immigration. He is married to Kate and they have one baby daughter, Ellen.

The tyranny of tolerance

In spite of contemporary Britain's diverse, pluralistic, post-modern culture, which rightly prides itself on its broad-mindedness and breadth of vision, the concept of heresy is alive and well. No matter how liberal a society is, it still needs boundaries, lines not simply of orthopraxy, or right action, but also of orthodoxy, or right belief. To belong, you need not simply to do the right thing, but to espouse the right beliefs. Much as we like to pretend otherwise, heretics, supposedly an extinct species, still remain, ushered out of public view so as not to threaten the notions of who we are and what we value.

In our more self-righteous moments, we protest at this survival. Heresy, we insist, is an archaic and authoritarian notion, ill-suited to our modern, tolerant world. At heart, however, we recognise that heresy is an entirely civilised and healthy fact of life. Anti-Semitic or racist beliefs are inherently dehumanising and should be unacceptable to any society of human beings. We may eschew the kind of thought police envisaged by George Orwell, or the overt propaganda of many twentieth-century secular, totalitarian states, but we achieve much the same effect by a tangle of laws, policies and social pressure. Holocaust denial may simply be a 'personal belief' but it is an incorrect and untenable one, which, rightly, denies the bearer full participation in society. Heretics are ostracised, if not quite excommunicated.

The problem with such subtle, modern forms of exclusion, however, is that they creep uninvited into many areas. Our current love affair with tolerance provides a somewhat ironic example of this.

To question the need for tolerance today is tantamount to questioning the roundness of the earth. The more fragmented a society becomes, the more important tolerance is. The decay of the Enlightenment project into postmodernity, and the collapse of the four historic pillars of Britishness – crown, union, empire and Protestantism – have atomised contemporary British society. Our answers to the big questions of identity, purpose and destiny now differ wildly.

Accordingly, our value systems vary significantly, as do the ways in which we choose to live our lives. In order to cope peacefully with this ideological and social fragmentation, we stress the importance of tolerance and emphasise the need to tolerate those with whom we naturally sometimes passionately disagree.

There is an incontrovertible logic to this. Only a fanatic or a lunatic would dispute the ever-growing need for ever-greater tolerance. Those who do so are subtly ostracised, a trend reflected in the fact that the word 'intolerant' is now not so much an adjective as a term of abuse. More often than not, to call someone 'intolerant' is to imply that they are antiquated, disagreeable and socially undesirable.

Supreme moral value

In spite of my provocative reference above to 'the tyranny of tolerance', I have no wish to question the need for tolerance, and still less to enter the fold of social pariahs. Tolerance, in so far as it represents a willingness to live alongside 'the other', is both morally right and politically necessary.

I do, however, want to question our contemporary, unthinking deification of tolerance and to point out that it can lead, and arguably has led, to a curtailment of personal freedom: something, ironically, that it was intended to protect.

Over recent years I have conducted a series of one-to-one and group interviews in my role as a researcher for the London Institute for Contemporary Christianity. These covered a wide range of topics but their centre of gravity was, broadly speaking, 'faith, doubt and living in Britain today'.

Without exception, tolerance was the supreme moral value of the people to whom I spoke. It was one of the few 'win-win' words in our modern lexicon, a little like 'community' or 'choice'. Everyone acknowledged its importance. Everyone bemoaned the fact that there was not enough of it. And everyone recognised that society needed more.

This should have been comforting. The message was clearly getting through. The more different we are, the more tolerant we need to be. My respondents' enthusiasm for tolerance boded well for the future.

Except that it did not, and rather than being comforting, the enthusiasm for tolerance was rather disquieting. Examining why revealed a (long-recognised) tension at the heart of tolerance, and several of the ways in which that tension manifested itself in contemporary British society.

It soon became clear that tolerance, rather like beauty, was in the eye of the beholder. The homage that was invariably paid at the altar of tolerance obscured the fact that tolerance was not, in actual fact, considered a universal good. It was possible to be *too* tolerant. One female respondent, for example, opined that 'all this business about being racist, I think it's gone a bit too far down the road . . . people can't actually say what they think any more for fear of upsetting someone'. Her comment sparked a mini-tirade from a number of fellow interviewees about 'political correctness'. Far from being confined to one person, the sentiment that 'it's all gone a bit too far' was widespread. Over the course of the various interviews I heard several examples, mostly concerning supposed policies of local councils towards ethnic minorities, cited as instances of how things had apparently gone 'too far'. Tolerance, it emerged, was not a single, obvious absolute value but, rather, a spectrum, which bordered 'intolerance' at one end and 'over-tolerance', or political correctness at the other.

Erosion

This complicated the picture. Tolerance, our supposedly universal panacea, was not, in fact, universal. This may at first seem to be a rather abstruse and academic point, of interest to moral and political theorists, perhaps, but irrelevant to life today, and unrelated to the task of preserving valued freedoms. In reality, however, it became the pivot and justification for a slow erosion of traditional freedoms.

During one of the groups, long after respondents had finished deifying tolerance and had moved on to talk about Christians and the church (the main focus of the research project), one young woman proclaimed to the group, 'I think they should ban the word church and they should ban the word religion.'

It was a rather careless comment. As a group, the respondents had long since finished talking about tolerance, and as an individual, it appeared, this particular respondent had long since finished thinking about it. A shift in topic and a moment of honesty had accidentally revealed her more profound feelings.

The comment was disquieting, however, not for its aggression or for its distasteful hypocrisy, but for revealing how the tolerance spectrum, as mapped out in her mind, debarred religion and religious practice. She, like her fellow interviewees, had acclaimed tolerance and preached its necessity, but implicitly drew its boundaries in a way that excluded 'church and ... religion'.

While her opinion may appear to be little more than bigotry, it had a deep, if rather paradoxical, logic to it. Because this individual recognised tolerance as the supreme moral good and the solution to most of the world's problems, those people who were deemed to be intolerant were, accordingly, seen as heretics who were part of the problem rather than the solution. In a wholly logical if rather crude move, their kind of intolerance was simply unacceptable.

The result was that the more intolerant people are (which essentially meant the more intolerant I judge them to be), the more intolerant I will be of them. The paradox will be obvious. The more people praised tolerance, the less like tolerance it became. Indeed, at its most extreme, there was a crypto-fascist element to some respondents' devotion to it. Tolerance easily became 'totalitolerance'.

Contorted logic

The implication this has for Christians or, indeed, others who choose to lead a consciously different lifestyle should be obvious. Under the cloak of tolerance, it soon becomes acceptable to deny the freedom of other groups, with the justification that they are intolerant. From this foundation of contorted logic spring the absurdities of evangelism being viewed as an 'incitement to religious hatred' or of university Christian Union groups being barred from Student Union membership for refusing to admit atheists onto their executive board.

The most notable recent examples of this 'totalitolerance' are continental rather than British. The French ban on the wearing of 'conspicuous' religious symbols in state schools was the topic of much debate in 2004. This ban on Muslim headscarves, Jewish skullcaps, Sikh turbans and Christian crucifixes was aimed at preserving France's ethos of secular tolerance, and although it was greeted with much hostility from the relevant faith groups when proposed, it was implemented with little protest. At the cost of limiting the freedom of these groups and in some small way eroding their identity, the objective of safeguarding the nation's secularist identity was met.

More recently, the new commission of incoming EU president José Manuel Barroso was rejected when MEPs from the liberal left objected to the appointment of Rocco Buttiglione as commissioner for justice, freedom and security. Buttiglione, a committed Catholic and moral conservative, had a controversial political record, and his statements on homosexuality, the family, asylum and immigration gave many cause for concern over his appointment. Yet, in his interview with MEPs he said, 'I may think that homosexuality is a sin but this has no effect on politics, unless I say that homosexuality is a crime.'

'The state has no right to stick its nose into these things,' he reasoned, 'and nobody can be discriminated against on the basis of sexual orientation ... this stands in the Charter of Human Rights, this stands in the Constitution and I have pledged to defend this constitution.' His insistence that it was possible for the personal and political to coexist while being at odds with each other was disregarded, in spite of the fact that it is one of the fundamental intellectual pillars of liberal democracy, and Italy's Prime Minister Silvio Berlusconi eventually withdrew him as his country's candidate for the commission. In an intemperate if honest article in *The Times*, Matthew Paris summed up the attitude of those who had rejected Buttiglione's appointment. 'I say: enough of tolerance. I do not tolerate religious superstition, not when it refuses to tolerate me. Sweep it from the corridors of power.'

Faith in society

For all their complexity and controversy, these two events were at least widely and openly reported. Matthew Paris was clear about his intolerance of Buttiglione's 'religious superstition' and the French ban, for all its pettiness, was at least official and authorised. There was no mistaking it for what it was: an attack, in the name of tolerance, on the liberty of those groups who, albeit in a minor way, do not conform to the societal norms. In a rather more tangled and less transparent way, Britain is stumbling in the same direction, without the 'benefit' of official endorsement. The result is that Christians (and others) who critique or bemoan this trend can be accused of suffering from a persecution complex and easily dismissed.

As with many such accusations, there is some truth in this. It is popular in some Christian circles to talk of a secularist or atheistic agenda, one that has developed or hijacked political correctness in order to eradicate all traces of Christianity from the land. While there is undoubtedly a coterie of hardline secularists and fanatical atheists who dream of a British public (and private) life from which the stain of 'faith' has been removed, they remain small and, in many cases, ineffectual. Any broader social analysis shows that atheism is widely dismissed and secularism of interest to few. When the British Social Attitudes survey last asked people about their belief in God, in 1998, only one in ten people agreed with the statement 'I don't believe in God', with the vast majority expressing some form of theism. When the Office for National Statistics revealed the results of their controversial faith group question in the 2001 National Census, it emerged that only fifteen per cent of people had said they had no religion, and only seven per cent declined to give an answer, despite the fact that the question was the only voluntary one on the form. Both atheism and secularism are minority sports.

Instead, political correctness has its roots in the genuinely positive desire to eradicate previously acceptable prejudices from the public sphere, and in this objective it has been singularly successful. A list of derogatory and dehumanising terms has been evicted from public rhetoric, for which the public square is a wholly better place. The method, it may be argued, is rather underhand and even tyrannical – better, surely, to teach respect than to hound disrespect from our vocabulary – but its success is to be welcomed.

Opportunity

The challenge – but also the opportunity – that presents itself to Christians today is that having helped clear the public square of racist and homophobic sentiments, a handful of enthusiastic progressives are attempting the same thing with faith groups, under the guise of inculcating much-needed tolerance across society. The challenge is obvious and other chapters in this book have explored the forms it takes in political, legal, educational and other spheres.

But the opportunity may be less obvious, and is worth pointing out. The grounds for evicting racism from the public square are reasonably obvious: racism dehumanises. The grounds for evicting intolerance are less clear. Tolerance, as we have noted, is woefully subjectively defined. It is not a universal good and that means that intolerance is not necessarily an evil.

Defending intolerance, like questioning tolerance, is heretical and yet, if only we can think our way through the social opprobrium that has accreted around the word 'intolerant', we will realise that every society needs to be, and indeed is, intolerant. Intolerance is the mark of a society where the moral horizons extend beyond me and my own. It is, in this respect, the mark of a humane society. A wholly tolerant society is an anarchy by another name.

Sometimes, regrettably all too often, we have been intolerant of the wrong things, whether that was Catholicism in the eighteenth century or atheism in the nineteenth. But just because British society has been intolerant of the wrong things in the past does not make intolerance itself wrong. We are most of us, thankfully, intolerant of child pornography, Holocaust denial and racial discrimination, because we recognise that each is, in its own way, pro-foundly dehumanising.

And it is this recognition that offers the opportunity for Christians. Because as soon as we realise that the world cannot be divided into two camps, of the tolerant and the intolerant; that, in reality, the tolerant/intolerant boundary runs right through each one of us; that intolerance is not a relic of a bygone age of bigotry but rather a useful, indeed necessary, social tool; in short, that properly speaking, tolerance is a *means* and *not an end*; as soon as we realise this, the topic of debate shifts from *whether* one should be tolerant or intolerant to *what* we should be tolerant or intolerant of, and why. And recognising this moves the focus from the rather monochromatic and insipid 'Do we need to be more tolerant?' to the more interesting 'What kind of society do we want?' What vision of individual human flourishing inspires our thinking? And what concept of corporate well-being shapes our policymaking?

This, it seems to me, is a rather more fruitful avenue to explore. It steers us away from a sterile debate about who is and who isn't sufficiently tolerant, a debate that all too often descends into rancorous squabbling and name-calling. And, accordingly, it steers us towards one in which agendas that are often hidden under a cloak of sweet-smelling words – choice, liberty, freedom, tolerance – are exposed.

Not only does it expose those submerged, driving agendas, but it also demands we justify them. It requires us not simply to spell out what we believe is and isn't tolerable but also to articulate why. And in such a debate a Christian faith, which, in Elaine Storkey's words, sees human beings as 'creaturely and not autonomous; dependent, not self-sufficient; relational, not individualistic; moral, not mechanical; unique, not mass-produced; accountable, not self-regulating; significant, not pointless; eternal, not temporal', has a lot to gain.

The alternative – of a society that grows intolerant in spite of, indeed because of, its uncritical homage to tolerance – is not appealing. That 'totalitolerant' society, in which tolerance is elevated from being a useful and necessary weapon in the armoury of civilisation to the position of a god whose righteousness cannot be questioned for fear of the wrath of its holy warriors, cannot help but limit the freedom its members. In doing so, it ironically and tragically fails to do the very thing it set out to accomplish.

As so often, Christ's words, albeit transposed from different circumstances, prove pertinent, in this case to a society that deifies tolerance. 'No-one can serve two masters. Either he will hate the one and love the other, or he will be devoted to one and despise the other.' You cannot serve both God and the god Tolerance.

Part 2

In-Depth Analysis

Academic Overview

Part 2 In-depth analysis

Chapter 11

The Legal Historian: Charles Foster

Charles Foster is a barrister, writer and traveller. At the Bar he practises mainly in medical law, and has been involved in many leading cases in recent years. He teaches Medical Law and Ethics at the University of Oxford. After reading veterinary medicine and law at Cambridge he researched wildlife immobilisation in Saudi Arabia. He was a Research Fellow at the Hebrew University, Jerusalem. The author of many books, chapters and articles on legal and non-legal subjects, he spends a good deal of his life on expeditions and writing. Charles is a member of Holy Trinity Brompton. He is married to Mary, a doctor, and they live in London.

Understanding the historical backdrop: law, freedom and Christian principle in England

The myth of Protestant heroic history

Modern Protestants seem to suffer from a highly selective historical memory. The new Christian revisionism says that Scripture contains some clear principles which, when translated into legislation, lead to just, compassionate and happy societies. These principles, say the revisionists, were lost during the dark ages before the Reformation, were rediscovered and dusted off then, and have been bringing joy ever since in those nations wise enough to permit their application. European history, according to this view, is a tale of faithful, Bible-reading heroes passing the blazing baton of truth one to another so that the world might see and live.

This view of history cannot survive a moment's view of the facts. For every slavery-abolishing evangelical Wilberforce there were a thousand impeccably orthodox evangelical slave masters. Humanists rather than Christians were in the vanguard of the movements for the emancipation of Jews, Catholics and women. The rhetoric of the early trades unionists might have been learnt in the non-conformist chapels, but its real appeal was to the naked self-interest of the workers. The smoke of burning Catholic martyrs is just as dense as the smoke of burning Protestants. Thomas More was murdered with just as much sincere brutality and brutal sincerity as was Ridley. Protestants knew how to use the rack just as well as the Inquisitors of Spain. And nobody but a madman or a masochist would want to live in Calvin's Geneva.

It is naïve to say that obscenities have been done in the name of Christ simply because the perpetrators did not read their Bibles properly. One person's honest exegesis is another person's equally honest anathema. It will always be so. Scripture is breathing as well as breathed: organic, variegated and complex. To treat it like a Romano-Germanic legal code is to misunderstand it.

It is often assumed that there is a blindingly obvious scriptural consensus about the principles of social justice. The books are full of respectful talk about the 'tension' between Paul's insistence that slaves be subject to their masters and Amos's assertion that oppression of weak minorities is intolerable to God. And no doubt they are right. But some other Christian ages were more ready to use the word 'contradiction' instead, and even those ages which thought that they could resolve the tension were less confident about how to resolve it than we seem to be.

So we cannot give Christians all the credit for the application of principles that we would now identify as Christian; nor can we blame non-Christians for all the barbarisms. All this is trite, but sadly needs to be said in a modern Christian book.

This means that a chapter describing the contribution of either individual Christians or Christian principle to the development and protection of civil liberties is really impossible. Too many questions are loudly begged: Who is a Christian? What is a Christian principle? Should a Christian principle deployed by a humanist be excluded? Should a humanist principle deployed by a Christian be included? The best that can be done is to draw a crude map showing the main milestones on the way to what we have in England today, and to make some broad-brush comments about why those milestones are there, and what Christian retrospection has to say about them now.

Law and ethics in the early church

The first Christians were not hugely interested in civil society. That was simply because they did not think it would last very long. Jesus was on his way back, and the urgent priority was to prepare for that. There were more important things to do than write laws. Christians were citizens of a celestial kingdom with its own set of laws. The society that Jesus had talked about was clearly not of this world. There was an obligation to render to Caesar, but not to discuss at length the equity of that rendering, let alone its mechanics. Paul urged slaves to submit to their masters, and the Epistles bristle with exhortations to the Christians to be compliant Roman citizens. We should be wary about labelling these exhortations as theological principles. Paul's concern was to ensure Christianity's survival and expansion. That could best be achieved, he thought, if Rome did not see Christianity as a threat. And the best way to achieve that was to direct the Christians to behave.

Christianity was ethically distinctive from the pagan world. Its ethical beliefs were basically those of Judaism, but in some ways more fastidious. Jesus, in the Sermon on the Mount, had introduced a whole new tranche of thought crimes: you murdered a man not just by stabbing him, but by being angry; you became an adulterer by mentally undressing a woman. Christianity's insistence on the reality of the afterlife, together with the supreme altruism of the cross, made Christians carelessly generous in their giving. The pagan world was baffled and impressed. Jesus healed, and bodies were important. Christians tried to heal, and again it was noted. Christians rescued and nurtured children exposed at birth: it was no more than pious Jews should have done, but it came to be seen as the uniquely curious behaviour of the followers of the Crucified Jew.

Perhaps the most distinctive characteristic of the Christians was not what they believed, but the fact that they acted. Altruism, compassion and generosity were valued highly in the non-Christian world. The literature of Greece and Rome is full of stories praising such virtue. But those tales are tales of mythical heroes, not of actual washerwomen. And the heroes tend to be altruistic in order to gain heroic status. Altruism, for the Greek, is an optional extra: a career-enhancing device for the would-be elite hero. In Christianity, washerwomen are altruistic unto death because there is a duty to love unconditionally. The Christian is not his own: he was bought with a price. A corollary of that transaction is that he owes duties to the wider world. Some of those duties were later to be crystallised into formal legal principles.

There is no doubt, too, that sheer fear of judgement played a part in Christian social impulse. If you feed the hungry, said Jesus, you are feeding Jesus himself. And if you don't, you are starving Jesus, and things will not go well for you on the Day of Doom. Yes, the Christians looked after widows and orphans; yes, they bathed lepers' sores. They were often genuinely good people acting altruistically, but it is foolish to deny that they regarded their actions as prudent eternal investments. Jesus peppers his great invitations with blatant appeals to long-term self-interest.

The church which was forged in the eastern Mediterranean was, then, a church that was not much concerned with government. Its primary concerns were pressing and other-worldly. It lived its life expecting the imminent return of Jesus. To wait for the Messiah in a desert wilderness, as the Essenes had, was not, however, a perceived option for most Christians. The fact of the Incarnation and the stern injunctions of Jesus about helping the downtrodden meant that proper Christian other-worldliness meant binding up the broken-hearted and helping the weak. Shrill in the ears of the early Christians were the words of the Old Testament prophets who had urged justice and had called down terrible judgement on the heads of those who exploited or ignored the downtrodden. But where to side with Amos meant to oppose secular government, the Christians were cautious. The church had to be concerned about its own survival and propagation, and Paul's policy of appeasement towards Rome seemed sensible. Even so, Christians were blamed by many Romans for civil disobedience and even for the decay of the empire. Eventually, of course, Constantine was converted and the Christians suddenly found themselves as the counsellors of the empire they had been accused of destroying.

In theory this was an opportunity to reassert the scripturally predominant strand of thinking about the relationship between the individual and the state – the Amos strand. This would have made it legitimate for the corporate conscience to question the pronouncements of potentates, and mandatory for individual consciences to do so. It would have facilitated the growth of an exegetically coherent Christian philosophy of government; it would have allowed Christians to claim, intelligently, that democracy was their invention. One can't sensibly derive democracy from any theology which believes wholeheartedly in subjection to one's rulers. The fudge which says, 'We are subject to the will of the majority' supports only the caricature of democracy of the primary school books. But the opportunity was missed. It was missed because, predictably, the new Christian heads of state harnessed Paul's dictum to plough their own political furrows. If you should subject yourself to a secular state for the sake of Christ, they said, how much more should you subject yourself to a Christian state. And so the dictum grounded a new Christian totalitarianism: a totalitarianism which was to enable Charlemagne to say, with apparent scriptural authority,

'Be Christian or die,' and which, transmuted into the doctrine of the divine right of kings, was to cause so many damaging convulsions in Europe.

Amos was not dead, but he was buried. The history of his exhumation is the history of evolving Christian thought about the limits of individual freedoms in the state.

The seeds of Christian England

When Christianity first sailed into England it came, more or less, as the pristine apostolic Christianity of the book of Acts. And the effect on thinking about society was, for a while, the same as in the ancient churches of the Near East. The church lived the Apocalypse, and that is not a good way to establish civil law. People with breathless Messianic expectations have no breath to make secular speeches.

This was to change. There were two main reasons for the change. First, time went on and Jesus did not return. The Christians began to realise that one could not behave as if secular society was unimportant when it seemed as if that society was going to go on for a while longer. And second, Christianity was, in England, hugely successful. Most of England was quickly converted. This had implications for government. If one was a tiny, beleaguered minority, one had at least the luxury of not having to worry about the tricky business of legislating, with all the shabby compromises which that often entails. But if your success has made you the ruler, you have to start worrying.

The Roman church had already learnt a good deal about the politics of power by the time the Pope despatched Augustine to England. His missionaries met and disputed with the rather more ethereal Celtic missionaries who had evangelised Ireland, Scotland, Wales and north and west England. And at the Synod of Whitby (664), the Celts capitulated. It was not just a theological capitulation – a petty squabble about how to calculate the date of Easter. The Roman church had entered into a marriage with the secular world, supposedly baptising it before the marriage was consummated. The Celtic church was behind the times: it had no truck with the world, and insisted that if the world wanted to be baptised, it had to come and live in monastic seclusion on an Atlantic rock. There was ultimately no contest. The pragmatism of Rome won the day. Whitby set the agenda for the next millennium: the church and the world needed to work together. The dictates of the church would inform the world, and vice versa. The kings of England were henceforward Christian. Sometimes that meant that the church could restrain some of the worst excesses of the kings; sometimes it meant that it participated in and profited from them. But notionally, although nothing was written down, England had a Christian constitution.

Augustine to the Reformation

One cannot talk meaningfully about the law of England until one can talk meaningfully about the Kingdom of England. It was not possible to do that until the Conquest. Before then, of course, disputes were resolved and decisions made, but the existence of tribunals does not begin to imply that they applied a consistent corpus of law. The more consistent tribunals acted in accordance with what they perceived as immemorial custom – custom which had itself grown up because it was believed to embody some idea of immemorial justice.

An English lawyer, in 1470, contended that the English common law had existed since the creation of the world. He was probably perfectly serious. He meant that it was based on natural law, the notion that the basic principles of justice – those which hold the universe together – have been written indelibly on the human heart. For a Christian, the writing is sometimes obscured by the consequences of the Fall, and the business of proper legal scholarship is to scrape away the obscuring encrustations and declare what lies beneath. This was a major theme in the legal thought of Christians from earliest times. Scripture might help in elucidating the details of the underlying pattern, but was scarcely necessary. The notion of natural law may well be Christianity's most enduring legal legacy. A natural lawyer from the Dark Ages would immediately feel at home with the American Declaration of Independence. But of course implicit in the notion of natural law is the concession that there is nothing unique about Christian ethics. The Christians might see the universal norms slightly more clearly than unbelievers (since grace has caused scales to fall from their intellectual eyes), but even honest unbelievers, trying to do the decent thing, will grope in the right direction.

The Romans left little of their highly developed law behind in England when they went home. Some Roman law filtered back later, particularly through the conduit of canon law, which regulated ecclesiastical life, but it was never, until very recently, very significant. The Norsemen left more: a procedurally sophisticated, harsh code, in which property rights tended to trump rights of life and bodily integrity. But it was left to Alfred, who almost united the English for the first time, to attempt the first tentative legislation. His legislation, however, and the efforts of those who followed him, made no attempt to define precisely the laws under which the English should live. The customary law, which became increasingly uniform as England became increasingly united, governed most of life. This, again, was the case until very recently. The idea that most law is found in statute books is foreign to England: it is a late import, and does not do well in the strange climate of these islands. It grew up in Rome, and flourished in Napoleonic France, and is producing some very curious jurisprudential fruit. The point of this is to explain that to look at the Christian influence in the law, it is not good enough to look just at the statutes. Most of English law has been judge-made law. That is a good thing. It means bespoke solutions to unique legal problems. The off-the-peg solutions given by inflexible continental codes look terrible and tend to chafe at the forensic crotch.

After the Conquest, England was united. It was that, rather than any uniquely Norman legal ideas, which make the Conquest so crucial. It established feudalism, which made it imperative to formalise the law of land tenure and with it, to some extent, the law which determined other parts of life. The church, by and large, was silent. It had plenty to say about the law governing its own affairs (Thomas à Becket lost his life for saying it too loudly), and canon law became immensely complex. But two assumptions made the church more or less hopeless as a legal watchdog. The first was the established but developing idea that law-making and law-executing kings were God's agents: Paul again. And the second was the idea of natural law: nothing much needed to be said about the ethics of law, because the laws were inscribed already on the lawmakers' consciences.

The earliest laws of England broadly enacted the Ten Commandments. They were the laws of a notionally Christian state, but little distinctively Christian compassion can be discerned in them. A society which hangs a starving man for stealing a loaf of bread cannot with a straight face be said to embody the much vaunted Judaeo-Christian respect for life. English lawyers have always had a nasty tendency to elevate the eighth commandment over the sixth.

There was no real protection of religious liberties. Jews were officially tolerated until their expulsion from England in 1290, but even before then the authorities condoned, and sometimes orchestrated, the systematic persecution of Jews. No other faith, apart from witchcraft, was an issue. Witches were burnt. When the Crusaders burst into Jerusalem in 1099, they waded knee-high through the blood of their victims. Muslims were killed because they had had the effrontery to occupy the Holy Land; Jews were killed because they had killed Jesus and stubbornly refused to acknowledge that he was the Messiah; Christians from the native churches were killed because they did not practise the Latin rite. The Jews look back to Crusader rule as the worst time in the history of Jerusalem since the destruction of the Temple. Muslims in the Middle East have a far better track record for religious toleration than the Christians.

It is traditional to celebrate Magna Carta (1215) as the cornerstone of English liberties. Its importance is often overstated, but it is undoubtedly very important, both for what it signified and for what it actually enacted. It signified the end of the belief that the monarch could do exactly what he wanted to do without reference to anyone else. Previous English kings had made written agreements about the way they would behave, but King John's signature on the Great Charter was famously different. He signed it because he was over a barrel. It was his signature or his throne, as the barons made clear. Monarchy would never be quite the same again.

Charles I's mistake was that he had forgotten what happened at Runnymede.

It is a long document: it runs to sixty-three clauses. In its conclusion John declared

> It is accordingly our wish and command that the English church shall be free, and that men in our kingdom shall have and keep all these liberties, rights and concessions well and peaceably in their fullness and entirety for them and their heirs, of us and our heirs, in all things and all places for ever.

The guaranteed freedom of the church proved to mean little: ask any abbot of any of the monasteries dissolved by Henry VIII. But some of the other clauses were more durable. Many of them founded and inspired really significant later laws. Amongst the most significant were Clause 38, 39 and 40. They read as follows

> 38. In future no official shall place a man on trial upon his own unsupported statement, without producing credible witnesses to the truth of it.

> 39. No free man shall be seized or imprisoned, or stripped of his rights or possessions, or outlawed or exiled, or deprived of his standing in any other way, nor will we proceed with force against him, or send others to do so, except by the lawful judgement of his equals or by the law of the land.

> 40. To no one will we sell, to no one deny or delay right or justice.

The European Convention on Human Rights really has nothing to add to this as a statement of the basic rules of forensic fairness. Later legislation built on it. The Petition of Right (1628) and the Habeas Corpus Act 1679 both rested on Clause 39. Amos would be pleased with these clauses. His legacy began to awake in England in 1215. Many of the remaining moral tussles in English law were concerned with extending to all the protection which Magna Carta gave specifically only to free men.

One of the characteristics of law is, or should be, its certainty. But certainty can mean inflexibility, and inflexibility can mean injustice. It was gradually recognised that the harshness of the law sometimes needed to be mitigated by simple, pragmatic fairness. By the middle of the fourteenth century there was a formal court in which this mitigation could be sought – the Court of Chancery. Its development was inspired by a distinctively Christian idea – the idea of grace triumphing over law. It would have been better if the equitable principles of the Court of Chancery had tempered the law in the law's own courts, but this was not achieved until law and equity were fused by the Judicature Act of 1873.

Although it is not possible to talk about even remotely representative government until about the time of the Civil War (1642–51), Parliament started to evolve during the reign of Edward I (1272–1307), and by the time of Henry VI (1422–61 and 1470–71), Bills required the assent of both the Lords and the Commons. Again, it would be nice to see the hand of passionate Christian activists in this evolution, but it cannot honestly be done. Parliaments were a cynical exercise in tokenism, designed to keep the country quiet by giving the people a well-insulated box in which to shout. The real attitude of the medieval establishment to the concerns of the common people is seen in the treachery and brutality with which Wat Tyler's Peasants' Revolt of 1381 was suppressed.

But although there were hardships, the courts acted as a real check to arbitrary power, and the average man was left to farm, trade, dance and worship as he wanted to. Unlike most continental countries, England regarded law as something to invoke when one had a problem, rather than as a seamless blanket covering all aspects of life. The English did what they wanted to do, provided the law did not specifically forbid it. In continental Europe, everything was forbidden except what the law specifically allowed. This unwritten but universally acknowledged principle was a more robust guarantee of real freedom than Magna Carta ever was.

Things were to get much worse. The generally benevolent feudalism of the Catholic Middle Ages gave way to the totalitarianism of early Protestant England. England was soon to learn to look at law as an oppressor rather than a saviour.

Reformation to the present

It was not just respect for Scripture and repudiation of indulgences that were imported from Europe at the Reformation. With them came some thinking about the role of law that was entirely alien to England. The Reformers thought that the whole of life should be conditioned by and subject to Scripture. They also thought that the gap between the secular state and the church should be narrowed or eliminated. Put those two ideas together, and the result is a tendency towards theocracy. Israel could be rebuilt – a nation state subject to nobody but God, but wholly subject to him. There was a contemporary model for such a state – Calvin's Geneva.

Kings did not sit comfortably in such a state: God had, after all, only granted Israel its kings reluctantly. Surely a truly Christian, New Testament state need have no such tawdry compromises. But the Reformers were canny: they knew that the best way to advance their cause in England was, at least at first, to get the king on board. In fact Henry VIII jumped on board himself, as a petulant refugee from the strictures of Rome's divorce laws.

Reformation Christianity was, in a sense, democratic. It emphasised the importance of the individual getting himself right before God. The emphasis in medieval Catholicism had been on salvation by being grafted into the church – an emphasis which was open to some obvious abuses. But as the individual conscience became the touchstone of religious correctness, and the Protestant work ethic highlighted individual responsibility for the individual's social and economic position, the individual was likely to demand, and be given, responsibility for the management of the society in which he was a crucial component. That, eventually, is what happened. The Reformers' desire that everyone should be able to read the Bible was democratically important too. Literacy is generally the herald of democratic demands.

The Reformation and the Cromwellian Protectorate (1653–59) which it inspired were terrible times for non-Protestants. They were the high water mark of religious intolerance in England. This is unsurprising. Since, for the Reformers, the Book gave the answers to all questions with implacable certainty, there was a positive religious duty to enforce the Book's dictates. And if the state was a religious state, enforcement meant enforcement by the state. Theological distaste for Roman Catholic doctrine was easily transmuted into distaste for Roman Catholic individuals. The call to scriptural purity often became a call for ethnic cleansing.

The Ten Commandments were relatively easy to turn into legislation. They dealt largely with things that one could see: murder, theft, and so on. No one in England had ever tried before to make laws enforcing the thought crimes of the Sermon on the Mount. But of course if Scripture was the ultimate arbiter of right conduct, and if Scripture had to be implemented, one had to legislate against unscriptural thought too. And that is what happened. Some nasty things crept onto the statute book between the last quarter of the sixteenth century and the last quarter of the seventeenth.

Cromwell himself was a believer in religious toleration. He did not press too hard the laws which made life so dangerous for non-Puritans, and he invited the Jews back to England. It was a great improvement on the capricious rule of the Tudors. But the most robust defender of the Protectorate has to acknowledge that from the point of view of basic liberties it was a disaster. Civil libertarians breathed a huge sigh of relief when Charles II sat on the newly restored throne. The Protestant experiment, conceived by its most zealous advocates as a highroad to a Lutheran or Calvinist state, had failed.

It was a great mercy that England was never fully reformed. Its Bible (ironically held up now as the touchstone of Protestant orthodoxy) is a mirror of the English Reformation itself. It was translated by a committee in which high churchmen, openly contemptuous of Puritanism, predominated. It was not designed to let God speak in the language of the taverns and workshops, but was written in language already archaic at the time it was written, intended to emphasise the continuity with the ancient order of Melchizedek. Other more prosaic English translations (notably the Geneva Bible and Wycliffe's version) held their place in the popular Protestant market for many years after the King James Version was published.

England's reformation was always a shabby, cynical business, driven (much more so than on the continent) by politics rather than theology. The Church of England was spawned from the lustful loins of a syphilitic wife-murderer. But that had its advantages. It meant that the English would always understand the relationship between church and state to be a complex, pragmatic one. There would be none of the terrible certainties of Geneva, in which the whims of government were seen as the will of God. Consequently God would be less defamed than in Geneva, and the relationship could evolve with changing political circumstances without the evolution being branded as godlessness. When theocracies fail, the faith they represent tends to be swept clean away with the government which embodied it. There was no danger of that in England. Because the Reformers had failed to create a fully Christian state, resentment of the state never became outright resentment of Christianity itself. Christianity remained mystically woven into the fabric of English government. Its influence was real, but had none of the soapbox stridency which would make it easy to identify as quintessentially Christian.

Although the religious upheavals of the sixteenth and seventeenth centuries did not make England suspicious of Christianity per se, England did become suspicious of religious and philosophical enthusiasm. The English love of understatement, born in its contempt for solemn French frippery during the Hundred Years War, was confirmed at the Restoration (1660). Paradoxically, of course, the Restoration was a time of almost unprecedented frilly flamboyance, but it was irreligious flamboyance; instinctive, reactive flamboyance. There was no philosophy in it: it was not saying anything other than that it was relieved. The Restoration and the years which followed took their cue from no sermon, political or religious. England was tired of being preached at, and her response to any moral imprecation was inversely proportional to the volume with which it was uttered. From then until the reign of Victoria the way to convince the English ruling elite of anything was to ask very quietly, as if you couldn't care less, and to avoid strenuously any scriptural footnotes. Christianity was still there, though, seeping into government, drip-feeding the national ethic with the precepts of Sinai and Galilee, gently making legislation more tolerant and humane. But little was done expressly in the name of Christianity, and when it was, it often paid Christianity a frankly satirical lip-service. The most genuinely Christian legislation has often been driven by the least ecclesiastically orthodox. That was the case for much of what went on in the law in the late seventeenth and the eighteenth centuries.

The English have generally been strenuously anti-intellectual, although they have often been very clever. They did not have much time for the careful, earnest debates of the continental Enlightenment. But some whispers of those debates crossed the Channel. Perhaps the most durable was the distinction between law and morality drawn by the arguably Christian Immanuel Kant. Pragmatic English lawmakers had recognised the distinction for centuries, but sometimes felt embarrassed about applying it. They were glad to have the support of a heavyweight Prussian brain.

The eighteenth century saw great waves of religious revival rolling through the land. Whitfield and Wesley undoubtedly started a revolution, but it was a revolution in the hearts and homesteads of the electorally impotent. It did not generally touch the ruling elite. And England was not interested in the type of secular revolution which sent France into painful spasm at the end of the century. England was weary of civil war: It knew what happened if you decapitated your traditions.

The nineteenth century was rather different. The national church became more closely identified with government than it had been since the Protectorate. Partly this was an artefact of imperial success. The British Empire stretched from the rising to the setting sun. To the British, with their peculiar historical myopia, the Empire seemed miraculous and eternal – a gift given by God to his chosen people, the English. London was the New Jerusalem. The chosenness of the English evidenced the favour with which God viewed England: it would be churlish not to re-enthrone him at the centre of national life. God had scratched the back of the English, and since the English were polite, they would scratch God's back in return. So the Bible once again thundered in the House of Commons, and the Church of England was re-established.

Once the Establishment had decided to be baptised, it was forced to take seriously the demands of other, more strident groups. If you say you acknowledge the authority of Scripture, you have to listen patiently to other people who couch their petitions in scriptural terms. Nonconformism was now a potent force among the working classes, and potentially troublesome. It talked, in colourful Old Testament language, of equality and equity. It had to be placated, but it was persistent and intelligent enough to be placated only with genuine progress. Some of the most constitutionally important concessions were extracted with the gun of non-conformist wrath pressed to the Government's head. The Industrial Revolution created new and imaginative ways to abuse workers; the evangelicals of England, equipped with the rhetorical power of Tekoa, did their best to mitigate the damage.

But they were not unopposed, and on the big issues – notably the Reform Acts (1832, 1867 and 1884), which did so much to enfranchise – unimpeachably mainstream Christians were equally vocal on both sides of the debate.

It is easy to paint a romantic Christian picture of Victorian England – an England in which well-fed orphans, seizing the opportunities of social and financial opportunity given to them by governments and altruistic philanthropists and commended to them by their enlightened Bible teachers, climb the slippery pole and march clear-eyed through life, dispensing wisdom to the benighted heathen of Africa, freeing slaves and healing the sick, before retiring to be the patriarchs of idyllic country parishes, beaming seraphically on the adoring serfs.

The fact that this picture can be painted is partly a tribute to the genuine contribution made by Christians to the improvement of nineteenth-century life, and partly a tribute to Christian propaganda – itself the product of Christian hypocrisy and self-regard. If you were rich, it was easy to believe in the myth of England as the New Israel. If you were poor it was laughable. But the legislation put in place (with very mixed motives) by the predominantly Christian Victorians allowed subsequent poor citizens to have a real voice and real freedoms.

The Great War (1914–18) was the end of a lot and the beginning of a lot. It destroyed the faith of millions – faith in God (how could he allow such suffering?); faith in the Establishment (they swilled port behind the lines and sent the working men to their deaths); faith in the church (it had insisted that this was a holy war, and there was nothing holy about Passchendaele); faith in the Empire and the chosenness of the British (the Empire had not tumbled, but it was badly shaken, and God did not seem to have showed much favouritism at the Somme); and faith in order (chaos had reigned, and none of the fixed points of the old world survived). But there was a new faith – faith in common humanity. The bodies of those common humans struck down in Picardy were to form the bridgehead to the brave new world. Damn the officers, damn the creeds of the regimental chapels: welcome to the new world of equality and self-created opportunity. There was a new proletarian Enlightenment, with legislation to match. Many of the laws which are now regarded as anchors of our fundamental freedoms were born in the era between the two world wars – notably the Equal Franchise Act 1928, which gave women voting rights equal to those of men, embryonic trade union legislation, and properly entrenched versions of the rights of lawful assembly. Not only was much of this not inspired by or endorsed by Christians, much was a product of the violent energy of repudiation which followed 1918 – a repudiation which expressly included rejection of the hold which Christianity had on national life. But Christianity was not sidelined so easily. Much of the morality of the secular reformers was learned in the Sunday Schools, or intuited by consciences which were basically Christian. England had been marinaded for over a thousand years in Christianity: if England pulled itself out of the vat, it was bound to reek of Christianity for a good while to come.

A similar phenomenon happened in the aftermath of the Second World War (1939–45): a sort of weary anarchy. But by now England was well and truly out of the Christian vat, and the winds of international change were beginning to dissipate Christianity's ancient aroma.

The historic rights of protest, assembly, habeas corpus and fair trial are of course important. They are what everyone thinks about when they talk about civil liberties. But the everyday freedoms of most law-abiding people are affected far more by another development: the growth of corporations. They are creatures of the last couple of centuries, but have grown monstrously and intrusively since the last world war.

Corporations ape individuals. The language with which they describe themselves is the language of human anatomy. Their organisation is the organisation of the body. They have asked for, and have got, freedoms which only individuals should be entitled to have. But limited companies are not made in the image of God. They do not have the conscience which should be a precondition to the possession of freedom. They are not subject to the illness and mortality which are a check to the ambitions of men. They are theoretically immortal.

If monopoly laws do not work, a tiny number of companies can rule the world. They can become more constitutionally important than governments. They write the laws of many lands. And even smaller companies can make demands of the individuals who depend on them which render irrelevant and practically impotent the freedoms which, in legal theory, are guaranteed to the individuals. The freedom of companies can be the slavery of individuals.

Looking at developments over the last quarter-century, three points need to be made: First, modern Christians seem to be weak without shaming the strong. They have to rely now on the laws which they (often) reluctantly conceded were necessary for the protection of minorities. Second, as Christians have gone more and more onto the back foot, they have begun asserting their rights. There are no human rights in the Bible. The notion is an Enlightenment one. The English common law, woven substantially from Judaeo-Christian threads, has never used the language of rights. It has preferred instead the language of duties. The most famous common law case, *Donoghue v Stevenson*, makes a lot of the law of tort turn on a question which Christians readily recognise. I owe a duty to my neighbour: who, then, is my neighbour? The House of Lords gave a more restricted answer than the Parable of the Good Samaritan did, but the emphasis is the same – an emphasis on obligation rather than entitlement. The European Convention on Human Rights, now grafted into English law and loudly relied on by many Christian lobbyists, is egocentric in its focus. 'What does the world owe me?' it asks. The Christian answer is: 'Nothing. But what can I do for you?' Autonomy is the light which the Convention uses to illuminate all human behaviour. Christians voluntarily forgo their autonomy. Of course being a servant is not to be a doormat, and of course it is important to be able to think and worship and preach. But we need to be careful. The rights culture is changing the way that Christians look at their relation to the world. And we need to wonder aloud whether a rights analysis really adds anything. The Convention has, by and large, been a colossal damp squib in the English courts. Duty-based common law did justice in the sense that the Bible aches for justice.

Third, and perhaps most significantly, Britain has for hundreds of years been a sufficiently mature democracy to prevent the tyranny of the majority – the danger inherent in the very idea of democracy. It seems to have lost that maturity. Ask the demographically irrelevant British countryside, which is now wholly disenfranchised and has its laws written for it by urban MPs – MPs who have no stake or interest in the countryside, but are nonetheless happy to sacrifice the freedoms of others on the altar of, at best, personal preference.

It does not do to get too political in a Christian book, but if there is any value in a chapter taking a long view of our basic liberties, it has to be said that the arbitrariness and unaccountability of the present Government has no precedent since the Tudors. No executive for four hundred years would have dared to treat Parliament (by which is meant the Lords and the Commons) in the way that our present executive has done.

When modern courts talk about Christian influence, they talk about 'the Judaeo-Christian tradition'. And they are quite right to use such a vague term. The influence of that tradition is easy to describe: the influence of Christianity itself is not. Individual Christians have sometimes secured, sometimes fought against, and sometimes availed themselves significantly of our basic liberties. Most of the people who have made the laws of England have been at least notionally Christian. Their minds and their language were often more Christian than they were. But their achievement should not be belittled. They made a corpus of law which is suffused with the Christian notions of duty, even-handedness and the protection of the weak. The law let the voice of the little man be heard, but stopped him becoming a tyrant.

The basic freedoms are under a more severe threat now than they have been for centuries. They are threatened not just by governments, but by the trend to uniformity which demands that everyone wears the same clothes, reads the same magazines, thinks the same, and ultimately is the same. These trends are powered by the legislation which allows monopoly. Babel is being rebuilt. This time there are many towers, and the headquarters are in California. Individuals are subject to and defined by huge corporations. Christians need be anti-corporate in the commercial sense, so that they can be properly corporate in the Christian sense – usefully contributing their own uniqueness for the good of the community. Christians need to stand for wild, unrestrained individualism (an individualism kept in dazzlingly creative tension with servanthood) – partly because they are called to have fun, and being the same as everyone else isn't fun; partly because being truly oneself is highly politically subversive; and partly because if the ancient laws which protect individualism aren't used, they will wither and die.

12

The Missiologist: Philip Meadows

Dr Philip R. Meadows is an ordained presbyter in the British Methodist Church. He was lecturer in theology and religious studies at Westminster College, Oxford, before spending six years as E. Stanley Jones Professor of Evangelism at Garrett-Evangelical Theological Seminary, near Chicago, USA. Now, Dr Meadows is serving as Director of Postgraduate Studies at Cliff College, Calver, specialising in missiology and the theology of evangelism, and is president of the Wesleyan Theological Society. His research and publication interests seek to combine theology and discipleship in the Wesleyan tradition with the missionary challenges of contemporary culture.

Understanding the mission field around us

Introduction

Jesus said, 'If you continue in my word, you are truly my disciples; and you will know the truth, and the truth will make you free' (Jn. 8:31–32, NRSV). He gave this advice to some Jewish leaders who had believed his messianic claim that he had been sent by the Father. But they did not understand this promise of freedom. 'We are descendants of Abraham and have never been slaves to anyone,' they replied. The freedom they treasured was the freedom to be a holy nation, God's own people, by obeying the covenant even when living under political tyranny. Jesus responds by challenging their ancestry, not their argument. The true descendants of Abraham, who are set free through faithful obedience to God, are those who love and follow him.[1]

Yet Jesus knows that the Jewish leaders' zeal for the law blinds them to the light that he brings, and will be the very ground upon which they seek to extinguish it from the earth. Ironically, they seek protection under the law from the one who is the very Author of it. The sin to which they are enslaved, and from which they need to be freed, is claiming a freedom before God that they will try to secure by putting his own Son to death. So, Jesus exposes the fact that the freedom they treasure is actually freedom from the hard truth that he brings and the radical discipleship that he calls for. It is a freedom born of the devil. It is only through the cross that this false freedom is finally exposed, and true freedom is revealed to be a matter of dying and rising with Christ, found in a cruciform pattern of discipleship.

In our claims about Christian freedom, we must not commit the sin of the Jewish leaders. The desire to secure our freedom as the birthright of a Christian nation, and to have it protected through the rule of law, has not advanced the cause of the Gospel in our day. Arguably, this approach has actually served to kill the church of Jesus Christ through the stealth of nominalism and the way in which it can release us from the call to radical Christian discipleship.

The issue is not whether Christians should insist upon the legislative freedom to practise their faith openly and without persecution. They should. At stake is the freedom that Christians have to follow Jesus with or without the protection of the state: a freedom for the obedience of faith that is only secured by the cross and resurrection; a freedom to live and die for the sake of the Gospel in the face of persecution. I will argue that a willingness to treasure and embrace this freedom, no matter under what political conditions we live, is the challenge to Christians in an increasingly post-Christian society.

It is a basic Christian claim that Jesus Christ is Lord of all. He is not just Lord of the church, but Lord of all creation, and this is the basis of our witness to the state. In the New Testament, the rulers and authorities of this world are manifestations of the 'principalities and powers' that shape the social, political and economic conditions under which human beings live.[2] These principalities and powers were originally created by God to order human life towards the good, which is the kingdom of God under the rule of Christ himself (Col. 1:15–20). He intended that the 'powers that be', and the governments they shape, should be subject to the lordship of Christ. In their present condition, however, they are neither inherently good nor evil but fallen and rebellious: created for goodness and holiness, but tending towards evil and injustice. A proper Christian response to the state and its government, then, is both obedience in so far as it is subject to the reign of God (Rom. 13), and resistance in so far as it rebels against its true purpose (Rev. 13).

For Paul, the rebellious nature of these fallen principalities and powers is revealed in the death and resurrection of Christ. By putting Jesus to death on a cross, the powers that be did their worst, extinguishing the life of the one for whom they were created. By defeating death through the resurrection, however, God secured victory over the principalities and powers, putting them under his feet (Col. 2:8–15).

The eschatological reality in which we live is that the fallen powers, though defeated, are not yet completely subject to the rule of Christ (1 Cor. 15:20–28). Until Jesus returns and finally draws all nations to himself, Christian freedom means living in the truth of his lordship amidst rulers and authorities that continue to be deceived by the powers that be. It is a freedom given by the resurrection power of God to live a life worthy of the calling to which we have been called (Eph. 4:1) in a world of unbelief.

The fallen powers always promise freedom of some kind, but the allegiance they exact from us typically works by deception: they blind us to their dominion by making worldly values seem self-evidently true. Christian freedom means receiving the truth of the Gospel, and the invitation to follow Jesus, as an alternative way of life which exposes our docility towards the powers that be and liberates us from their subtle influence. The freedom we have in Christ is a freedom to discern where our habits of thinking, feeling, speaking and acting have been held captive to the ungodly mores of the dominant culture. Indeed, it is only when we are confronted with the radical alternative of Christian discipleship, and discover our reluctance to embrace it, that our bondage is made evident.

Christian freedom is to be loosed from the tutelage of this world through binding ourselves to the teaching of Jesus and 'continuing in his word'. Discipleship, therefore, involves unlearning many of the worldly habits we have unwittingly absorbed, habits that we have even confused with Christian life itself. In what follows, I want to expose some of those habits, not least the way we have come to think of, and treasure, the idea of freedom itself!

Freedom and obedience in a culture of democracy

The democratic ideal of freedom in modern culture has its roots in the Enlightenment's commitment to universal reason and moral sense. Immanuel Kant defined the nature of the Enlightenment as freedom from 'tutelage', or the discipline of external authority

> Tutelage is man's inability to make use of his understanding without direction from another. Self-incurred is this tutelage when its cause lies not in lack of reason but in lack of resolution and courage to use it without direction from another. . . . 'Have courage to use your own reason' – that is the motto of enlightenment.[3]

Kant and his successors hoped to free society from the capricious authority of religious institutions by founding the moral life in the use of human reason alone. Whatever one thinks of institutionalised authority, the idea of rejecting any authority that cannot be located within oneself should be very disturbing to us. Christian discipleship is precisely the opposite: to yield our lives to the strange authority, teaching and discipline of Jesus our Lord.

The legacy of the Enlightenment has been a commitment to personal autonomy (literally, being a 'law unto oneself') and individual freedom, such that each does what is right in his own eyes (cf. Prov. 12:15). The all too familiar 'virtues' of modern freedom are self-determination ('I choose my own way of life'), self-sufficiency ('I can make it on my own'), self-satisfaction ('I don't need anyone else'), self-creation ('I will be a self-made man/woman'), and self-possession ('I dispose of my life the way I see fit'). In modern liberal democracies, these constitute a freedom to direct the course of our own lives, to choose our own ends, and to pursue them as we desire. It is as though we are capable of standing on some neutral ground above all the claims of the world upon us, and the principalities and powers that shape daily life.

When we are confronted with the Gospel, however, it turns out that the apparent freedom of choosing one's own end – or what constitutes the 'good life' – is really a form of bondage to the deeply individualistic and self-interested powers of modern culture. Consider the summons of Jesus: 'Follow me!' This invitation to discipleship is neither a question nor an option but a command; the very issuing of it denies the possibility of neutrality. Either we will follow, or we will not. So, for example, the rich young ruler's unwillingness to follow Jesus revealed the extent of his bondage to worldly self-interest (Mk. 10:17–22), not the capacity for free choice. The freedom of a Christian does not lie in a general capacity of choice but in being confronted with a particular kind of choice: specifically to deny self by following Jesus (Lk. 9:23–24).

The invitation to unconditional obedience reveals exactly who, or what, is lord over our lives. On the one hand, the self-centred virtues of modernity represent desires that are cultivated and rewarded by our consumerist economy and the political institutions that embody it. On the other hand, Jesus made self-denial and taking up the cross a condition of authentic discipleship because the new way of life to which he calls us requires putting to death an old life shaped by the powers of self-interest. By inviting us to take up our cross and follow him, he offers us freedom from a culture that enslaves us to our sinful desires. The more tightly we bind ourselves to Christ as Lord, the more we are loosed from the powers that be.

So, what is 'the freedom we treasure'? Is it the freedom of liberal democracy? A freedom to pursue self-interest, to determine the course of our own lives? A freedom to take or leave the teaching of Jesus in so far as it serves our own ends? Or do we treasure the freedom that authentic discipleship brings? A freedom to receive the gift of our true end, which is loving communion with the triune God, now and for ever. A freedom to approach God as 'Abba, Father', being set free from the guilt and the power of sin. A freedom which the Spirit brings by indwelling our hearts and gathering us into Christian community where we watch over one another in love.

Truth and goodness in a culture of violence

It is claimed that contemporary culture is increasingly suspicious of 'metanarratives' – the 'grand stories' which those in authority tell to support their claims to truth and what constitutes the good life.[4] For example, the ideals of liberal democracy arise from the stories which modernity has told about individual autonomy and the 'myth of progress'. The Enlightenment confidence in universal reason and moral experience gave birth to an optimism that humankind, once it was freed from the superstitions of institutional religion, would find common agreement upon the nature of truth and goodness, and usher in a brave new world.

Modern culture has certainly freed us from religious authority, but this optimism has not been well founded. For all its scientific discovery, technological advancement and economic prosperity, the common cold is still a killer, the art of war grows increasingly violent, and poverty still ravages the world. Closer to home, our local communities have been dismantled, family life is increasingly dysfunctional, and our personal lives are more lonely and fragmented than ever. This postmodern generation is right to be sceptical about the stories of modernity and their overconfidence in human nature.

It would seem, however, that truth abhors a vacuum and postmodern philosophers have rushed in to fill it with stories of their own.[5] They say all claims to universal truth are nothing more than the 'will to power', or useful social fictions which enable those in authority to manipulate the lives of others. They say all claims about the moral life simply mask this violent abuse of power, and the history of Christianity proves it. What is needed, therefore, is the 'therapy of deconstruction'. Cultivating a life of suspicion becomes a means to freedom from the many violent claims made upon us by persons and institutions alike. In this way, the individualism of modernity is perfected through the postmodern intuition to 'trust no one' as the only way of escaping bondage to other people's self-interest and their power over us. Suspecting that the truth is not 'out there' brings a sense of freedom to construct reality for oneself, and become a player in this 'matrix' of competing truth claims. Postmodern freedom situates us somewhere between victim and victor among the powers that be, and in our relationships with others.[6]

Critics like to point out that the assertions of postmodernity actually constitute a new kind of meta-narrative with its own universal truth that there is no universal truth! Worse, however, is the implication of 'ontological violence', or the conclusion that conflict is an inescapable fact of human existence.[7] The age-old myth of 'redemptive violence' – that one kind of violence can only be redeemed by another – has seized this postmodern nihilism and permeates contemporary culture like the air we breathe. The books we read, the video games we play and the movies we watch all relentlessly draw us into a world of violence where goodness is embodied by heroes who slay the enemy to secure a promising future.[8]

Yet here is the ambiguity of postmodern culture. In principle, we are against the use of violence for fear of becoming that which we detest. In practice, we are resigned to its inevitability, and thankful when the 'powers that be' turn to violence in order to secure the so-called 'freedoms' we enjoy. Indeed, closer inspection reveals much of our daily lives to be shaped by a fear that others are potential enemies, and the belief that we must do everything in our power to defend ourselves and remain in control of our own destinies. This combination of suspicion, distrust and violence threatens to infect all our relationships: at home, at work, and even in the church.

Sadly, many Christians have perpetuated this myth by interpreting the atonement as an act of redemptive violence willed by God to defeat the violence of human sin. Closer inspection of the Gospel story, however, reveals Jesus to be one who redeems the world by refusing the violence of worldly power. The first disciples are told to love their enemies, Peter is rebuked for his use of the sword, and the true meaning of Jesus as Messiah turns all military expectations of violent revolution upside down.

In the midst of deadly persecution, the pacifism of the early church was inspired by Paul's interpretation of the atonement as the victory of Christ over the principalities and powers.[9] Death has lost its sting and violence is overcome for those who follow Jesus and share in his radical witness (literally, as 'martyrs') to the peaceable kingdom of God.[10]

As we have seen, Jesus promised that we would know truth and freedom by trusting him enough to stake our lives on his word. This invitation to place our lives in the hands of another in the face of an unknown future comes as a profound challenge to postmodern ears. We find ourselves identifying with those would-be disciples of Jesus who prefer to negotiate the terms of discipleship in advance, only to be summarily dismissed as unfit for the kingdom of God (cf. Mt. 8:22; Lk. 9:62). We would rather make strategic plans, and depend upon our own power to make them come out right, than to embark on the adventure of a discipleship which defies our ability to be in control.

The summons to follow Jesus, and our unwillingness to embrace it, exposes our captivity to a life of suspicion, even though experience tells us we cannot make it on our own. The faith which Jesus calls forth cannot be founded upon our fears and doubts, as real as they may seem, but only upon a confidence that our lives are in the hands of one whose love refuses violence, yet whose power works all things for the good of those who love him.

So, what is the freedom we treasure? Is it the freedom of postmodern suspicion which we gain by distrusting those around us? A freedom to determine truth and goodness for ourselves, secured by the myth of redemptive violence? A freedom to negotiate with Jesus the conditions of discipleship before staking our lives on him? Or do we treasure the freedom that authentic discipleship brings? A freedom from the nihilism and violence of contemporary culture. A freedom to live peaceably with our neighbour through radical trust in the providence and grace of God. A freedom which the Spirit brings by gathering a community of non-violent love which is capable of healing our broken relationships and the worldly divisions of race, gender, ethnicity and social status.

Justice and love in a culture of toleration

After the English Reformation, religious toleration meant the possibility of non-conforming traditions finding a lawful place alongside the established church. In the seventeenth century, the Act of Toleration meant that Presbyterians, Congregationalists, Baptists and Quakers, for example, were free to register their own buildings, license their own clergy and hold their own 'opinions' regarding doctrine, modes of worship and church governance. The toleration afforded by the established church was to be mirrored by a rejection of bigotry among the non-conforming churches themselves. In the eighteenth century, John Wesley summarised this religious tolerance in his notion of the 'catholic spirit', or the possibility of being committed to the fixity and truth of one's own commitments while still relating with justice and love to those who differ.

The ground of this catholicity, however, was a common commitment among Christians from different traditions to the lordship of Jesus Christ. It was not meant to solve the contemporary problem of religious pluralism, or how Christians should live alongside persons of other religions, be they Jews, Muslims, Hindus or Buddhists. In more recent times, liberal democracy has held out a principle of religious freedom that adapts well to this situation, by making all religious commitments a matter of private opinion and removing all religious communities from the realm of public life. In other words, religious freedom has been secured by 'privatising' the church and subjecting it to a secular politics which refuses to authorise any religious claim as public truth.[11]

The church, having enjoyed an historic place of privilege in national life, has willingly embraced this arrangement as a means of securing its own primacy over other marginalised religious voices. In the ruins of a post-Christian culture, however, it is finding itself to be just one more religious voice being silenced by the politics that formerly established its influence.

The tolerance of liberal democracy retains a flavour of the old catholicity in so far as it recognises the freedom of private institutions to have exclusive commitments to truth and goodness, and to recruit others so long as they do not transgress public polity along the way. Evangelism has been the subject of scorn rather than prohibition, and censured only by the church's own lack of proper confidence in the Gospel. With the emerging conditions of a postmodern culture, however, the evangelistic task of proclaiming the Gospel as public truth comes under suspicion as an act of violence against those of other religions.

This suspicion is intensified by the ambiguous history of an established church which still occupies a formal place of privilege and power. Notwithstanding the general demise of Christendom, the enemy still portrays the church as a threat to social harmony in a way that other religious groups do not. Indeed, it is ironic that the church suffers increasing marginalisation at the hands of a government which continues to establish it as a national institution.

The 'new tolerance' is no longer a matter of acting with justice and love toward those who differ. It is now about refusing to claim any uniqueness or finality for the Gospel, and unconditionally affirming the claims of truth and goodness made by others. So, we are pressed to think of 'truth' as just one group's version of reality, 'goodness' as just one group's version of the moral life, and religious freedom as the power to choose for oneself what is true and good.[12]

Some Christian thinkers have claimed that this postmodern pluralism represents different approaches to the same transcendent spiritual reality and/or different manifestations of the same inner spiritual experience. It is no coincidence, however, that such thinking has become the new orthodoxy for a privatised spirituality that suits the ideals of liberal democracy and our consumerist economy. To critique this pluralist agenda is virtually an act of religious and political heresy. What appears to be a commitment to religious freedom and toleration is actually a primary allegiance to certain philosophical and political ideals that subordinate all other claims to truth, including the Christian Gospel.

So, again we ask, what is the freedom we treasure? Is it a religious freedom secured by the privileges of established Christianity? A freedom protected by government legislation that silences competing voices? A freedom to proclaim the Gospel without opposition or persecution? Or do we treasure the freedom that authentic discipleship brings? A freedom from the privatising forces of contemporary culture. A freedom to strive for the Gospel as public truth in a world of unbelief. A freedom for evangelism when missionary service amounts to a form of civil disobedience. A freedom which the Spirit brings by gathering a community of truth that is willing to live the Gospel with or without the protection of the powers that be.

Conclusion

There are three possibilities facing the church in this kind of post-Christian culture. First is to retreat – to form Christian enclaves and leave the nation to its own devices. Second is to retrench – to strive for a new Christendom or a renewal of established Christianity's privilege and power. Third is to radicalise – to understand the 'signs of the times', strive for authentic Christian discipleship and community in a culture of unbelief, and participate in the mission of God to proclaim the lordship of Christ through evangelism and social action, whatever the cost.[13]

In my view, what our nation needs is radical Christian communities which seek to embody the truth and freedom of the Gospel in their life together: to be in the world, but not of the world, for the sake of the world. This kind of Christian freedom is a challenge because we have been largely deceived and domesticated by the principalities and powers. The challenge of Christian freedom is to resist the temptations of liberal democracy, redemptive violence and privatised religion in so far as they appeal to our sinful self-interest and lure us away from the rule of Christ.

The church is authorised by the lordship of Christ, and set free by his Spirit, to live an alternative way of life as a witness to the state – obedient to the state in so far as it is an instrument in God's hands, but resisting the cheap freedom it offers and choosing instead the costly discipleship which Jesus requires of us. We need to recover our apostolic vocation 'to make everyone see what is the plan of the mystery hidden for ages in God who created all things; so that through the church the wisdom of God in its rich variety might now be made known to the rulers and authorities in the heavenly places' (Eph. 3:9–10). It requires an intentional and daily commitment to the virtues of self-denial in a world of self-interest; trust and faithfulness in a world of suspicion and violence; and radical public witness in an unbelieving world that would silence our voice. How we accomplish that is the real adventure of true Christian freedom and discipleship.

---

[1] For a detailed study of St Paul's approach to freedom and obedience in the Christian life, see John Barclay, *Obeying the Truth: A Study of Paul's Ethics in Galatians* (T. & T. Clark, 1988).

[2] This biblical theme was recovered by a number of theologians in the aftermath of the Second World War (e.g. Jacque Ellul, Karl Barth) and has figured prominently in the work of John Howard Yoder. For a helpful summary, see Marva Dawn, 'The Biblical Concept of "Principalities and Powers" in Stanley Hauerwas et al. (eds.), *The Wisdom of the Cross* (Eerdmans, 1999).

[3] Kant, Immanuel, 'What is Enlightenment?' in *Foundations of the Metaphysics of Morals and What is Enlightenment?* (New York: Liberal Arts Press, 1959), 85.

[4] See the classic work of Jean-François Lyotard, *The Postmodern Condition*, tr. Geoff Bennington and Brian Massumi (University of Minnesota Press, 1984).

[5] For an account of nihilism in postmodernity, see Gianni Vattimo, *The End of Modernity* (Polity Press, 1988).

[6] Most of these themes are addressed in the opening chapters of J. Richard Middleton & Brian J. Walsh, *Truth is Stranger Than it Used to Be: Biblical Faith in a Postmodern Age* (IVP, 1995).

7 See John Milbank, *Theology and Social Theory* (Blackwell, 1993), ch. 10.

8 See Walter Wink, *The Powers that Be* (Doubleday, 1999). This volume is a summary version of his theological trilogy on the principalities and powers. His analysis is very helpful despite rejecting a biblical view of the powers as personal beings.

9 For a classic study of this theme in the theology of atonement, see Gustaf Aulen, *Christus Victor* (Wipf & Stock, 1993).

10 The root of the English word 'witness' is to be found in the Greek *marturia*, from which the word 'martyr' is derived.

11 See Lesslie Newbigin, *Truth to Tell: The Gospel as Public Truth* (Eerdmans, 1991).

12 Wesley rejected this kind of 'latitudinarianism' as the spawn of hell, not the offspring of heaven!

13 See Rodney Clapp, *A Peculiar People: The Church as Culture in a Post-Christian Society* (IVP, 1996).

13

The Philosopher: Talal Debs

Talal Debs is a Research Associate at the Centre for the Philosophy of Natural and Social Sciences and a Visiting Fellow in the Department of Philosophy, both at the London School of Economics and Political Science (LSE). After receiving his PhD from Cambridge University in 2001, Dr Debs was a Postdoctoral Fellow at Harvard University and has taught philosophy at the LSE and the American University of Beirut. He has published in the history and philosophy of science, especially the philosophy of modern physics.

Understanding the philosophy of our time

Nothing new

Addressing the impact of the 'philosophy of our time' on Christianity today is a tall order, especially through the medium of a short essay like this. The first challenge is to determine what is distinctive about the current intellectual climate. It has often been said that there are few if any truly new ideas. An eloquent expression of this is found in the words of nineteenth-century philosopher Friedrich Nietzsche, intended as a criticism of the work of other philosophers

> . . . how unfailingly the most diverse philosophers always fill in again a definite fundamental scheme of possible philosophies. Under an invisible spell, they always revolve once more in the same orbit; however independent of each other they may feel themselves . . . Their thinking is in fact . . . a homecoming to a far-off, ancient common-household of the soul, out of which those ideas formerly grew . . .[1]

Of course, these words are particularly ironic in the light of the fact that this very observation has itself been made countless times. Over two thousand years before Nietzsche, the biblical writer of Ecclesiastes could claim with no less poetic flair

> What has been will be again, what has been done will be done again; there is nothing new under the sun. Is there anything of which one can say, 'Look! This is something new'? It was here already, long ago; it was here before our time (Eccles. 1:9–10).

While there may indeed be nothing entirely novel about the philosophy of our time, in reality, each age has its own distinctive mix of ideas that have a degree of currency. Thus it is still a worthwhile task to inquire into the distinctive philosophical trends of the age. We will focus on one such trend.

Before we do, it is worth asking what sort of current ideas might count as philosophical. The word 'philosophy' itself means 'the love of wisdom' when translated directly from its Greek roots, and philosophers have long pursued both wisdom and truth. Philosophy so understood is not the exclusive preserve of 'professional thinkers', and if there is a 'philosophy' of twenty-first-century Britain, it should include popular attitudes to both truth and wisdom. That is to say it informs twenty-first-century men and women as to what kind of things are true and what kind of things they ought and ought not to do.

Diversity

Understanding popular attitudes towards truth and morality in modern Britain, and in the West generally, is complicated by the fact that this society is fantastically diverse. This diversity is evident in the various beliefs held by members of an increasingly heterogeneous culture, ethnically, religiously and in just about any other sense one can consider. There may well have been other eras of human history that were equally diverse, first-century Mediterranean culture perhaps, but characterising what today's diversity shares is nevertheless no simple task.

One place to begin, however, is with the concept of a liberal society. According to John Gray,[2] modern 'liberalism' has been distinguished by four key themes:

- Individualism: valuing the individual over the group;
- Egalitarianism: insisting on equal value of individuals under law and in codes of moral conduct;
- Meliorism: social and political institutions must undergo continuous revision and are not expected to converge on an ideal;
- Universalism: according 'moral unity' to all humankind.

These themes have to a large degree shaped the way that people in the West evaluate public morality. Laws and other codes of conduct are often directly or indirectly assessed according to criteria based on these assumptions. As Gray argues, however, the foundation of modern liberalism may not be sufficient to manage the realities of so-called 'postmodern' culture. In philosophy, postmodernism, according to the well-known phrase of Jean-François Lyotard, is marked by 'incredulity towards metanarratives'.[3] Thus, the postmodern thinker is consciously sceptical of any larger story that provides an interpretation for particular events in our lives. Both truth and morality are entirely relative to culture, and are in effect cultural illusions. With this attitude it is especially hard to see how the modern liberal insistence on the moral unity of humankind could be maintained.

Certainty

This postmodern attitude did not develop in a vacuum. It was in some sense a reasoned, though perhaps ultimately inadequate, response to the competing claims to certainty made by rival cultural groups within our diverse society. These include those whose worldviews have been shaped by science, numerous religious traditions, or other so-called 'forms of life'. From living with this evident conflict, the conviction emerged that the problem of these clashes of certainty is not to be found in the specific claims made by one group or another but in the very notion of objective certainty in the first place.

This has caused many to ask: where does any certainty come from? Or even more to the point, can we ever get it without becoming fools or oppressors or both? Finally, the postmodern thinker is led to wonder: is it somehow wrong to want certainty? But since answering 'yes' would commit the postmodern 'sin' of certainty, the consistent postmodern thinker is more likely to settle on the conclusion that the desire for certainty is simply intellectually immature or childish. But this leaves individuals in a dilemma, suspicious of certainty but longing for it nonetheless.

To put a human face on this, one might consider the case of Edward Said. In his haunting memoir, *Out of Place*, Said chronicled his very personal story of being unable to live within any of the metanarratives on offer, that of being a Christian, an Arab, a Palestinian or an American. He concluded that he personally was 'out of place' among any of these identities as they are usually defined. The surprise, if there is one, is the wistful tone that he takes in expressing this fact. This is echoed in the way in which people in the modern West deny the meta-narratives that would give them identity but at the same time long to be located within a larger story that gives their lives purpose. Satisfying these conflicting drives is no easy task.

Total tolerance

One attempt to do this that runs deep in western culture is by applying an ethic of being 'true to oneself'. The self is put forward as the sole guide for moral choices. But if an act is considered right or wrong solely on the basis of its correspondence with individual conscience, moral judgements cannot help but be relative. This reality manifests itself in the oft-repeated phrase, 'Well, that may be true for you, but my truth is different.' In addition to this radical relativism at a personal level, the ethic of being true to oneself has been used as a guide to public morality in the form of what might be called the ethic of total tolerance.

This ethic of total tolerance has recently been dubbed 'totalitolerance', and was one of the principal findings of a recent market survey of attitudes in mainstream modern Britain

> Tolerance was the unquestioned supreme deity in the respondents' universe of values. Intolerance the greatest sin. . . . Tolerance, was, however, in the eye of the beholder, with each individual drawing the boundary [between intolerance and political correctness].[4]

Thus the purportedly universal moral imperative to tolerate others' views and actions must itself be relativised to the individual in order to avoid an obvious contradiction. In other words, insisting on an unvarying public ethic which demands tolerance of certain views and rejection of others would at times be in conflict with the personal ideal of being 'true to oneself'.

But how far does a relativised universal ethic, which sounds like a contradiction in terms, take one as a real guide to making moral choices? To answer this question, let us first state succinctly what the moral of total tolerance might require: one must in all cases tolerate the views and actions of others, *and* one's own views *and* actions must always be tolerated by others.

On first reading, this sounds eminently sensible and even like an application of the famous Christian ethic commonly referred to as the 'golden rule'. It is after all only applying the condition to treat others with tolerance as one wishes to be tolerated oneself.

Dilemma

An obvious problem exists for the ethic of total tolerance if and when one is faced with beliefs that are held
to apply generally. This can lead to a situation in which
a violation of the ethic of total tolerance is guaranteed.
Consider a case in which two people, A and B, hold
beliefs that purport to be universal but upon which they
disagree. To take a contentious but very current example, when A believes that female 'circumcision' ought to
be carried out on all women within their community
but B believes this activity, though traditional to A, is
objectively harmful and ought not to be required of
anyone.[5] Both A and B are likely to cite strong reasons
for believing that their different views of right and
wrong are each universal or at least generally applicable. In this case, if one encourages either party to adhere
to the ethic of total tolerance they are faced with a
dilemma. If A tolerates the views of B, A must accept
that his or her own beliefs are wrong. If instead A insists
on their own view being tolerated, they must at the
same time insist that B's beliefs are wrong. Thus either
one or the other of the two conjuncts of the ethic of total
tolerance stands violated. This situation will pertain
any time two or more people disagree over what they
hold to be universal claims. A further complication is
caused by the fact that the ethic of being true to self is
generally deemed to be more fundamental than the
ethic of total tolerance, so each person will tend to
retreat from the latter only to insist that their own right
to be tolerated must be defended.

How might one get out of this predicament and
still respect the ethic of total tolerance? One obvious
step might be to limit the sense in which tolerance extends to beliefs with potentially universal

application. To stay with the example above, one might suggest that both parties should modify their view of the situation so that their moral imperatives apply only to their own community. Thus, A can believe that all female members of A's community should be 'circumcised', and B can believe that all members of B's community should not. In this way it appears that both A and B can hold their views and tolerate the other without the dilemma which arose before.

But in reality this apparent harmonisation is only possible if A and B define the term 'community' in the same way. In particular, they must define their community in a way which is mutually exclusive and upon which they both agree. If either A or B defines their community differently, perhaps by cultural affiliation or heritage, a situation could easily arise in which those claimed by one as members will also be claimed by the other. Thus, for example, B may consider their community as defined by being citizens in a liberal democracy and A may consider their community as being defined by a cultural or religious identity. Assuming that B wishes to consider at least some members of A's community as being part of their liberal democracy there is an overlap between these groups, and A and B will each face a similar dilemma to that encountered already. Accordingly, if A believes that all female members of A's community should be 'circumcised', and B believes that all members of B's community should not, they are once again at loggerheads, this time over the status of any individuals who are claimed by both communities. So, each party once again has the choice of tolerating the other's view or abandoning their own, and the ethic of total tolerance still stands violated.

Assumptions

So, in order for the ethic of total tolerance to hold one must first of all restrict general beliefs to statements that apply only to one's own community and secondly all parties (not just A and B) must agree on the designation of who is part of what mutually exclusive community. This is a pretty strong restriction, but it gets worse. In reality, of all the possible ways to determine who is part of what community there is only one that does not lead to a violation of the ethic of total tolerance. The communities to which A and B consider their beliefs about female 'circumcision' to apply must be defined as the groups of people who share their respective beliefs. Even if we are told that A and B agree (on the basis of cultural heritage) that a given woman is part of A's community and therefore should be circumcised, if she does not believe this herself her own views have not been tolerated, and the ethic of total tolerance has been violated on her behalf. Similarly, if A and B agreed (on the basis of being a citizen in a liberal democracy) that another woman was part of B's community and therefore should be barred from circumcision, she might consider this intolerant towards her views if she did believe in the practice.

What this suggests is that the only general beliefs that can be tolerated (on the basis of the ethic of total tolerance) are those that do not apply to anyone who does not share those beliefs already. Thus, in the example above, person B will never be able to find a tolerant basis on which to reject female circumcision as morally wrong in all cases. By contrast, person A will be able to argue on a tolerant basis that it is morally right in the case where the woman in question believes it is right. In other words, the ethic of total tolerance reduces entirely to personal moral intuitions. The ethic of total tolerance claims to be a public moral and to provide principled guidance on how to live harmoniously in society, but in actual fact it gives no further guidance than the injunction to be 'true' to one's own beliefs.

The only way that the ethic of total tolerance can appear to provide more is if assumptions are smuggled in. As a result, tolerance is often erroneously cited as a justification for positions that on closer inspection are in fact intolerant themselves. In practice, people often do condemn the attitudes and behaviour of others, often on the expressed appeal to tolerance. But as we have seen, in order to do this they must in fact be basing their position on more than just tolerance, since the ethic of total tolerance is simply equivalent to the right to be true to oneself. We have seen that both A, the supporter of female 'circumcision' for all members of a given cultural community, and B, the opponent of female 'circumcision' for all members of a liberal democracy, are in violation of the ethic of total tolerance. So while A may have reasons to believe that female circumcision is generally a good thing, to claim they are not being tolerated by B is disingenuous since they are not tolerating B's position either.

Victim mentality

A practical outworking of the way in which the appeal to intolerance is used is what might be termed a 'victim mentality'. By assuming that the ethic of total tolerance is generally applicable, when in practice it is almost always violated, many people are in a position to claim that they are not being sufficiently tolerated. Since, moreover, no other ethic is as generally accepted, this is

often the only publicly acceptable way to express dis-
agreement with a moral view or practice. Thus, the
weighing of the competing claims comes down to
the subjective degree to which each party has suffered
at the hands of intolerance.

Taken to extremes this victim mentality would mean
that the only basis for a public hearing of a moral claim
might be a perceived or actual instance of persecution.
Returning one final time to the example of female 'circumcision', we have seen that both A and B are in violation of the ethic of total tolerance. Thus they might each
claim to be the 'victim' of the other, having suffered
intolerance. At this point any public discussion intended
to justify one claim or the other might easily turn on
who is perceived to have suffered more. The point at
issue would not be evaluated directly on the merits of
competing arguments but would be assessed through
the distorting lens of a victim mentality.

How does this affect the Christian church and other
groups whose very business is making general claims
about life, the universe and ultimate reality? The philosophical climate of the times makes it very difficult to
address moral issues in a principled way. This applies
to the church as much as to other institutions. Tolerance
in itself is not an ethic beyond the obvious point that we
are each free to believe as we actually do. This freedom
of conscience does not imply a moral free-for-all in the
way that the ethic of being true to oneself does. Nor
does it amount to a statement about what views or
actions must be tolerated. Indeed the Christian categories for this type of decision have to do with a
balancing of truth with love, or objective standards with
grace, and of general revelation (in the form of moral
intuitions) with specific revelations provided in
Christian scriptures.

Christian approach

The message is not that there are easy answers provided in the Christian scriptures for all moral dilemmas, but that the ethic of total tolerance is no help whatsoever in discovering them. Conflict of ideas and beliefs is unavoidable when more than one human being seeks to be 'true to self' at once. This reality has led many to despair of the lose-lose proposition that living in community often appears to offer – very few people indeed are truly able to find fulfilment in being 'true to self'. One classic example of this lament is found in the short modern classic *Civilization and its Discontents*, penned by Sigmund Freud in his final years. By this time racked with physical pain, Freud eloquently and bitterly represents the view that society offers us a devil's bargain whereby we deny certain of our true drives in order to gain a modicum of relief from others. Freud's pessimistic view makes a powerful argument for the futility of life when understood as primarily about the satisfaction of human drives. Given this observation, supported by the various miseries of human society as recorded in our history, the moral appeal 'to be true to self' should ring with irony rather than be the basis for a generally accepted public ethic.

The ethic of total tolerance represents a major trend in the philosophy of modern Britain, especially with regard to public standards of morality. Although it has its basis in an aversion to certainty in any field of inquiry, science, history, religion, etc, this is especially problematic in the ethical sphere. The ethic of total tolerance is of very little use in helping us manage the very real ethical dilemmas that face us today. The specific challenge to Christians is to persevere with and represent our own distinctive moral approach within the diverse 'market place' of ideas on offer in modern society. This approach has no more eloquent expression than the exhortation to 'Love the Lord your God with all your heart and with all your soul and with all your mind . . . and . . . love your neighbour as yourself' (Mt. 22:37–9). If it is taken to heart, much more good can be accomplished through this ethic than through the victim mentality engendered by the drive to be 'true to self' at all costs.

---

[1] Nietzsche, Friedrich, *Beyond Good and Evil*, Chapter 1, Section 20.

[2] Gray, John, *Liberalism* (Open University Press, 1995), xii.

[3] Lyotard, Jean-François, *The Postmodern Condition: a Report on Knowledge* (Minneapolis: University of Minneapolis Press, 1984).

[4] Spencer, Nick, *Beyond Belief: Barriers and Bridges to Faith Today* (London: London Institute for Contemporary Christianity, 2003), 20–21.

[5] The term 'female circumcision' is a controversial term since it implies an analogy with male circumcision, but unlike male circumcision it always results in loss of functionality of the organs affected. Because of this, critics of the term have suggested the term 'female genital mutilation' is more descriptive; the author has chosen to use the less contentious of the two terms in the text.

Epilogue

Steven Cotton and Clive Frampton

Two Christians, one (Steven Cotton) a teenager and the other (Clive Frampton) newly retired, provide the epilogue for this book with a biblical perspective which should be integral to any discussion of Christian freedom. Clive, a chartered surveyor, is married to Gwyneth, with four children and one grandson. He is a trustee of a number of trusts including Share Jesus International and the Deo Gloria Trust. Steven is a volunteer worker with Share Jesus International. He is hoping to do a degree in Theology and English and to pursue a career in writing.

Understanding the challenge ahead

Focused on Jesus

When thinking about persecution and the challenge of disintegrating freedom, we inevitably look towards the persecuted church in countries such as Vietnam and

Laos and in many other distant parts of the world. The images of imprisonment and torture begin to circulate in our minds. Yet in recent days it has become clear that the issue of persecution is a topic far closer to home, and that we, as Christians in the West, will become increasingly aware of it.

We do not know whether or not in the future the Western church will suffer torture and imprisonment, but there is an ominous atmosphere growing among many Christian workers. We have heard people say many times, 'There is something amiss. Society seems to be disintegrating.' Christians in general seem to sense that the spiritual battle is becoming more intense, but appear unable to articulate just how this is happening. Some believe that the added pressure on many Christians today is the first indication of outright persecution.

The question is, where do we go from here? The first step is certainly hearing God's voice – whether directly or through others – but then a decision must be made and we must decide what to do with what we have heard and learnt.

Jesus told his disciples, 'If any of you wants to be my follower, you must put aside your selfish ambition, shoulder your cross, and follow me' (Mt. 16:24, NLT). The same challenge is very true for us today. Our eyes must focus on Jesus. We must give God what is rightly his, and give the principalities and powers what is rightly theirs. In all things we must seek justice and truth; we must not compromise the faith nor fail to keep the promises we have made to Jesus Christ. Being a follower of Jesus is not a hobby or a part-time job; it is a life. We cannot feign faithfulness in times of prosperity and then turn our back on God in times of struggle.

Faithful in hardship

With God's Spirit living within us we have nothing to fear. In Micah 3:8 we read, 'But as for me, I am filled with power and the spirit of the Lord. I am filled with justice and might.' It is essential to hold on to the promises that God has given us. Through God's Spirit living within us we are strengthened, and 'the word of God is full of living power. It is sharper than the sharpest knife' (Heb. 4:12, NLT).

God has given us authority in prayer and we, as his people, must never abandon that. It is important to pray for suffering Christians everywhere, and it is important to pray for our persecutors. But praying for the leaders of our nation is often a more neglected practice. We must constantly give all of our concerns to God and seek his guidance; without God guiding us we are incapable of acting with love and authority, with confidence and yet with grace.

Paul taught us that to suffer for Christ is a great privilege: 'For you have been given not only the privilege of trusting in Christ but also the privilege of suffering for him' (Phil. 1:29, NLT). If we stay faithful to God through times of hardship he will surely bless us, and if the church remains rooted in Christ we will see it prosper.

'Be happy if you are insulted for being a Christian, for then the glorious Spirit of God will come upon you,' said Peter (1 Pet. 4:14, NLT). In times of trial God will equip us; his Spirit will strengthen us and he will be there with us. As we become smaller, God becomes bigger. We must remain rooted in Jesus and be focused on him as we live in the fullness that God has promised.

The apostle Peter's letter to God's people, who were scattered throughout the area covered by modern Turkey, was written during a time of great danger for the church. Persecution had accompanied the preaching of the message of freedom in Jesus Christ from the beginning. However, this opposition did not stop the spread of the good news across the ancient world.

In any discussion on the limiting of freedoms it is fitting to read what Peter was saying to those who had every cause to fear for their safety. Peter was facing a time of real persecution and suffering for preaching that Jesus Christ had been raised from death, and yet he was able to remind his readers of their spiritual inheritance (1 Pet. 1:3–12) and encourage them. He listed four practical ways in which they should conduct themselves in their difficult circumstances.

1. Hold on to your faith (1 Pet. 1:10–21)

God's revelation of himself in Scripture is unique; the prophets attest it and it culminates in the death and resurrection of Jesus Christ. The benefits of his suffering are far-reaching and are experienced by all those who believe in him. The past has been dealt with and the future is assured while the people of God hold on to their faith. In order to do this effectively it is necessary to be holy, as he is holy. This is the antidote to fear.

'Who is going to harm you if you are eager to do good? But even if you should suffer for what is right, you are blessed. Do not fear what they fear, do not be frightened. But in your hearts set apart Christ as Lord' (1 Pet. 3:13–15a). When Jesus is given his rightful place in our lives, there is no cause to fear.

2. Obey the powers that be (1 Pet. 2:13–15)

Peter exhorts his readers, 'Submit yourself for the Lord's sake to every authority instituted among men . . .' These words have caused controversy for Christians through-out the centuries. Even Peter and John questioned the Sanhedrin when it commanded them not to speak or teach at all in the name of Jesus. They explained that they could not help but speak the truth (Acts 4:19).

Perhaps we should be guided here by Jesus' words, 'Give to Caesar what is Caesar's, and to God what is God's' (Mt. 22:21). We should remember that Peter was living in a pagan society whose Caesar was considered a god, yet even in these circumstances the early Christians were urged to obey the powers that be. The reasons that are given are firstly that this should be done 'for the Lord's sake', and secondly that 'by doing good' they would silence ignorant critics (1 Pet. 2:13, 15).

3. Prepare to live as servants of God (1 Pet. 2:16–21)

Peter continues, 'Live as free men, but do not use your freedom as a cover-up for evil; live as servants of God.' In practical terms, Christians are urged by Peter to be ready to explain the reasons for their faith. This involves prayer and study and being immersed in the Scriptures so that a balanced message is given. Its presentation should be marked by respect and sensitivity to those who hear.

The servant of God should be prepared to do God's will, and be disciplined and focused on the ultimate purpose of God's grace. 'Therefore, prepare your minds for action; be self-controlled; set your hope fully on the grace to be given you when Jesus Christ is revealed' (1 Pet. 1:13).

4. Exercise the gifts of grace that have been given (1 Pet. 4:7–11)

There is no greater joy that a follower of Jesus can experience than to do God's will and exercise the gifts of grace that have been given to them. It is a completion of the circle – the sinner and outcast is restored by God's grace and is empowered by that same grace to continue Christ's ministry on earth.

With application and discipline we develop as servants of God and discover the ability to pray more effectively and to learn to love our fellow Christians of whatever persuasion more fully. In this way we can become what we should be – a loving community, offering new life in Christ to all in a sympathetic and relevant way – a beacon of hope in an increasingly despairing world.

Although freedoms may be threatened, there is no danger to the person whose life is hidden with Christ in God. This sense of security which God gives will enable all of his people to fulfil Christ's mission on earth, the purpose of which is that people everywhere should be saved and come to a knowledge of the truth. This is an opportunity to make all people free.

We close with a prayer:

> O God, the author of peace and lover of concord,
> to know you is eternal life,
> to serve you is perfect freedom.
> Defend us your servants from all assaults of our enemies;
> that we may trust in your defence,
> and not fear the power of any adversaries;
> through Jesus Christ our Lord.
> Amen.[1]

---

[1] *Alternative Service Book* (1980).